# The Faith Challenge

*30 Days to Deeper Intimacy with God*

**Dr. Theron D. Williams**

*The Faith Challenge*
*30 Days to Deeper Intimacy with God*
by Dr. Theron D. Williams

Printed in the United States of America

ISBN 9781613792469

www.xulonpress.com

# Dedication

*From God through me to you with Love!*

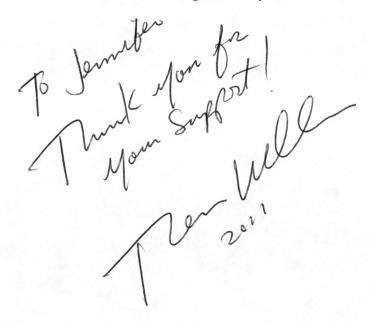

# Table of Contents

# Introduction

God called Abraham and instructed him to leave his kindred and his father's house and move to a land that God would show him. At 75 years of age, Abraham packed his things and moved, as God had directed him. From that point on Abraham enjoyed a deeply intimate relationship with God. He actually talked with God, fellowshipped with God, and even rejoiced with God. His relationship with God had grown so intimate that he was called *the Friend of God* (James 2:23 KJV). The term friend here is the Greek word *philos* which literally means companion. The inference here is that God and Abraham enjoyed deep familiarity and a sacred closeness that can only be experienced by two people who totally trust each other.

The Lord *appeared* to Abraham and announced that He was going to give to Abraham's offspring the Promised Land. Then the Lord spoke to Abraham again and told him to look to the north, east, south and west, and as far as his eyes could see, and declared to Abraham that that is the territory He had prepared to give to Abraham's offspring. The Lord God Himself is the One who changed his name from Abram to Abraham.

Abraham had such profound intimacy with God. He enjoyed this intimacy with God without the benefit of sacred scripture, without being part of a regular worshipping community, without having a spiritual leader, or without attending a workshop to inform him how to develop a relationship with God. All Abraham had was intimacy with God.

The intimacy that Abraham enjoyed with God also purified Abraham's "spiritual field." Everyone emits a spiritual field that is simply the outer projection of the inner spiritual state. People whose inner spiritual states are polluted with negative energies like anger, jealousy, sadness, rage, the need to judge, etc., often emit a negative spiritual field. Conversely, people who embrace positive energies like love, joy, compliments, happiness, forgiveness, etc., often emanate a positive spiritual field. It is the positive spiritual field that, like a magnet, attracts all good things into one's life. The negative spiritual field tends to attract only more negativity into one's life.

Abraham's intimacy with God sanitized his spiritual field and put him in the position to attract good things into his life. Thus, he became wealthy, famous, and blessed, and everyone who blessed him God blessed. Everyone who cursed him God cursed (Genesis 12:2-3 KJV). He was blessed with great health, so much so that he remained sexually active even at the age of 100. The deeper we move into intimacy with God, the clearer our spiritual fields become, and the more attractive we become to life's positive things.

Moses had an encounter with God while he tended his father-in-law's flock on the backside of the desert. God literally spoke to Moses out of a bush that was burning, but would not burn up. The Lord engaged Moses in a long, drawn-out conversation in order to convince Moses that he was the man God had chosen to lead His people out of bondage in Egypt. At first, Moses was not convinced that he was fit for the task as he begged God to select someone else. But God insisted and even went so far as to allow Moses to participate in two miracles to prove to Moses that He was indeed the God of his fathers, Abraham, Isaac, and Jacob. He instructed Moses to throw his shepherd's staff to the ground, and it turned into a serpent. Moses was then told to grab the serpent by the tail as it turned back into a staff in Moses' hand. The Lord told Moses to place his hand inside his cloak, and his hand turned leprous. When God instructed him to place his hand back into his cloak, his hand returned to normal. These were impressive magic tricks, but Moses was still not impressed enough to willingly take the job. The Lord became angry with Moses when Moses complained that he was not an eloquent speaker. He advised Moses to employ his brother Aaron who was an effective communicator. God promised that He would be with them to guarantee their success. (Exodus 3:1-4:31 KJV)

This conversation between God and Moses was so intense and intimate it was enough to carry Moses through a tough 40-year ministry. He didn't have a spiritual leader to preach to him and to instruct him in the Word. Moses simply had an intimate relationship with God.

His intimacy with God transformed his spiritual field. His sterilized spiritual field attracted numerous victories and successes into his life. Moses' leadership style has been the topic of many books and the model for leadership training workshops. Although Moses' leadership methods may be duplicated by others, they will never experience his successes unless there is an accompanying transformation of the spiritual field that comes as a result of an intimate relationship with God.

The Apostle Paul did have the Holy Scriptures, several worshipping communities to which he was connected and spiritual leaders, yet Paul understood that these were only to facilitate his intimacy with God. Paul had a personal encounter with the resurrected Christ on the road to Damascus. Paul actually heard the voice of the Lord saying, "Saul, Saul, why do you persecute me?" (Acts 9:4 NIV).

When Paul preached the gospel in Corinth, he was met with violent opposition. Obviously, Paul was apprehensive about continuing the work in Corinth because of this opposition. Then one night the Lord spoke to him in a vision to encourage him, saying, "Do not be afraid; keep on speaking, do not be silent. For I am with you, and no one is going to attack and harm you, because I have many people in this city" (Acts 18:9NIV). As Paul sailed to Rome to stand before Caesar, the ship met with a storm and was about to break up.

The passengers feared for their lives, but Paul had a divine visitor in the night who promised him that no lives would be lost and that he himself had to stand before Caesar (Acts 27:1-44KJV). Paul also recounted how he was taken up into paradise, and while there "heard inexpressible things, things that man is not permitted to tell" (II Cor. 12:4 KJV). Paul reminded the Lord of how he suffered with a thorn in his flesh. He asked the Lord three times to remove it but the Lord answered, No. He told Paul that His grace was sufficient.

Throughout Paul's ministry he enjoyed deep intimacy with God. He used the Holy Scripture, the church, and spiritual leaders as means to move him into closer relationship with God. Like the others, his intimacy with God purified his spiritual field. Thus, he attracted great success into his life as a preacher, church planter, theologian, and writer.

The level of divine intimacy that was enjoyed by Abraham, Moses, and Paul, and other biblical personalities can be enjoyed by everyone. In fact, it is God's desire that all might enter into this same level of intimacy with Him. Today we have an advantage that those of old didn't have. We have the Word of God to inform us, the church community to encourage us, the teaching of the Word to enlighten us, and preaching of the gospel to challenge us. God has provided everything we need to facilitate the process of moving us into deeper intimacy with Him.

I discovered the power and comfort of divine intimacy through an unexpected crisis that occurred in my life. In 2006, I went to my cardiologist's office for a routine stress test. The technician hooked me up to the EKG machine and conducted an ultrasound test before I was to start on the treadmill. Upon viewing the ultrasound and EKG results, the technician hurried from the room to notify the cardiologist of what the ultrasound revealed. The cardiologist came into the room and informed me that I had an aneurysm in one of my heart arteries, a dissected aorta, and a heart valve that was in such bad shape it was leaking blood. Open heart surgery was the only answer. This came as a total shock to me because I was extremely healthy. I had never smoked a day in my life. I hadn't eaten beef or pork in 20 years. I had just become a "quasi-vegetarian." I had been swimming one mile at least 4 times per week and did weight training three times per week. I didn't drink hard liquor and I got proper rest every night. I thought, "This is not supposed to be happening to me." I had worked so hard to prevent it. But there I was, preparing for open heart surgery. The surgery was scheduled to last 8 hours, but it ended up being a 13-hour procedure.

Praise God, the surgery was a success! The whole ordeal came at me so fast that I didn't have a chance to really reflect upon how severe and life-threatening my injuries were. I was released from the hospital after 13 days. When I returned home, it all hit me! I became obsessed with asking myself unanswerable and disturbing questions such as, would I completely recover? How long will I live? Would my life ever return to normal? I would often play mental movies about my future, which were always negative and very troubling.

I wanted peace but couldn't find it. I went to the Word of God but could not find the level of peace that I needed. After three months of recovery at home, I returned to church, hoping to find the peace that I so desperately needed, but couldn't find it there either. I listened to CDs of some of the world's greatest preachers, and still could not find peace. The Bible, the church, and the preacher had come through for me in other times in my life when I was desperate for peace and reassurance. However, it was discouraging this time to discover that the things I had relied on time and again for peace seemed to have failed me.

Late one night, while lying in my bed of affliction in dreadful despair, my 17-year old son, who was also looking for peace because of my ordeal, came into my bedroom. I had been his rock, his hero, and for him to see me in this condition sent him into a state of depression. He was devastated even at the thought of losing me. He asked me to explain the meaning of Psalm 42:7-8 KJV: "Deep calls to deep in the roar of your waterfalls; all your waves and breakers have swept over me. By day the LORD directs his love, at night his song is with me— a prayer to the God of my life." The moment I read the passage, my burden was miraculously lifted. This passage spoke to me in a way that the Bible had never done before. I knew experientially exactly what Isaiah 61 meant, for in that instance I received "beauty for my ashes, oil of joy for my mourning and a garment of praise for my spirit of heaviness" (Isaiah 61:3 KJV). This passage said to both my son and me that if one is to experience the *love that the Lord directs to us by day* and to *hear his song by night,* the deeper dimension of one's being must connect with God at a deeper and more profound level. I then understood that God allowed this situation into my life so that I might develop a deeper hunger and thirst for Him. I had always had God in my life, but now I needed more divine fellowship. The Bible wasn't enough; I needed that to which the Bible points. I needed more than the Twenty Third Psalm; I needed the Shepherd of the psalm. I needed more than an intellectual understanding of the Word, I needed an experiential encounter with the divine realities to which the Word points. I needed deeper divine intimacy with God. I longed to be God's friend. I knew that the peace I sought could only be experienced through deep intimacy with God.

As I moved into deeper intimacy with God in search of peace, I discovered far more than I ever imagined. It was as if God used my longing for peace to lure me into divine intimacy with Him; to expose me to a dimension of Himself that I never knew existed. My journey into deeper intimacy with God is characterized by a progressive enlightenment, through the continual unfolding of divine revelation. I no longer view life as one long continuum of events that are totally unrelated and meaningless. I now know that there are no coincidences, happenstances, flukes, luck, or chance. Paul writes that we all have one God who is, "Above all, through all and in all..." (Ephesians 4:6 KJV). Since God is in all things, it is only through Him that we realize the connectedness of all things and thus the purposefulness of life. Life now makes much better sense to me. Have I figured out all the mysteries of life? Of course not. Am I still puzzled and befuddled by certain things that happen in life? Yes, I am. But what comforts me is knowing that everything that happens is like a puzzle piece that fits perfectly within the divine scheme of things.

I started my journey with God decades ago with a destination on my itinerary. But my "upgraded understanding" of God revealed that my journey with God has no destination, it's an open-ended pilgrimage that takes me deeper and deeper into Him. An eternal God has no ending and neither does our journey in Him, and that's the essence of eternal life.

I have a far more profound appreciation for the Bible, the preacher and the church, because they ceased to be ends in themselves, but rather means to a greater end. That is to move me into deeper intimacy with God. I now enjoy God in a way that I had never known before. My fellowship with God is now even more real than my fellowship with people. I immediately recognize His voice and follow it as it leads me into peace, love, success, and prosperity. I embrace the love He *directs towards me by day,* and I sleep in peac*e by His song by night,* even in the midst of chaos.

I was taken totally by surprise with the other benefits I experienced as a result of entering into deeper intimacy with God. My entire spiritual field has been transformed. My spiritual field had been encumbered with negative energies like grudges, anger, pain, and the need to complain and judge. These negative energies had been blocking the blessings that I needed in my life.

Now, my grudges and anger have been replaced with love and forgiveness. My pain and disappointment have been transmuted to bliss and deep peace. Because those negative energies have been eliminated from my life, my spiritual field has been cleared and now the desires of my heart manifest into my life almost effortlessly. Literally, everything I need miraculously manifests. It doesn't matter if it is money that I need, a certain person or people with the knowledge, access, or expertise I need, even if it's a book or information I need, everything tends to find its way into my life to bless me. This is what Jesus meant when He said "Seek ye first the Kingdom of God and His righteousness and all of these things shall be added unto you" (Matthew 6:33KJV). This is the way life was intended to be lived.

One of the greatest challenges that Jesus faced was to enlighten His followers that the Scripture, tradition, laws, doctrine, and teaching are only tools to move people into personal and intimate relationship with God. And if the believers are not careful, these "tools" will end up preventing them from cultivating their relationship with God. In His effort to convince His followers to embrace this idea, His detractors accused Him of trying to abolish the Law and the Prophets. He tried to persuade them that He had not come to destroy the Law and the Prophets, but that they might be fulfilled. The Law and the Prophets are fulfilled when they are successful in moving people into deep intimacy with God. The religious leaders' mishandling of the Law and the Prophets actually created more distance between the people and God.

We are confronted with the same challenge today. When we fail to understand that the true purpose of the Holy Scriptures, the church and spiritual leaders is to facilitate our journey into a deeply intimate relationship with God, they end up being more of a hindrance than a help. I often find people who know the Bible better than they know God, and have a closer relationship with the church than they have with God, and are more committed to their spiritual leaders than they are to God. The Holy Scriptures, the church, and spiritual leaders are sign posts that are designed to point believers beyond themselves to a deeper spiritual reality.

When the Holy Scriptures become an end itself it certainly will lead to *Biblio-idolatry*, that is, worshipping the Bible rather than the God of the Bible. When one stops at the Bible and never moves to where the Bible points, one renders the Bible ineffective. The Apostle James puts it best, "Do not deceive yourselves by just listening to his word; instead, put it into practice. If you listen to the word, but do not put it into practice you are like people who look in a mirror and see themselves as they are. They take a good look at themselves and then go away and at once forget what they look like. But if you look closely into the perfect law that sets people free, and keep on paying attention to it and do not simply listen and then forget it, but put it into practice - you will be blessed by God in what you do" (James 1:22-25GNV).

A fellow clergy colleague often tells the story of a man who served in the office of Deacon at the church before my colleague assumed the pastorate of the church. He recalls this man as one of the most faithful men at the church. The members would often reminisce about how he took out a second mortgage on his house and donated it to the church to make up for the shortfall that the church needed for the down-payment for the new church building the church wanted to purchase. He volunteered to clean the church when the church could not afford a janitor. He would work his 8-hour job during the day, and would come in during the evening to clean the church. He led the charge against one of the former pastors to have him dismissed, because he was guilty of embezzling hundreds of thousands of dollars from the church over a 4-year span, and he was also guilty of molesting several teenage girls in the church. The current pastor acknowledged that this deacon was very instrumental in getting him hired. His love for the church was unquestioned. He was not the kind of man who had to have everything go his way at the church, and he often supported the pastor by following his leadership. He had been credited with squelching many a church squabble that could have easily escalated into full-fledged church conflict. Once, during a revival, the pastor called on this deacon to lead the church in prayer. He refused to pray but gave the responsibility to another deacon. When the pastor inquired of the other deacons why this particular deacon refused to pray, they all said they didn't know and that they had never heard him pray. They had never known him to teach a Bible lesson, never heard him quote Scriptures, mention the name of Jesus, make any references to God. In the month of March that following year the pastor preached a series of sermons on salvation. The last Sunday of the month the pastor preached from the Gospel of John 3:16, on the topic "You must be born again." At the conclusion of the sermon this man who had been a deacon for twenty years and loved the church, came to the front of the church and for the first time in his life, accepted Jesus Christ as his Lord and was saved. With tears in his eyes, he told the church that one of the church's old pastors saw that he was a young, energetic man and out of the blue one Sunday morning after church, called him into his office and made him a deacon. He said he had not accepted Christ and didn't understand who God was, but since the pastor asked him to serve he thought he had no choice. He said the reason he never offered public prayer is because he had never prayed before. The reason he never attended Bible study or taught a Bible class was because he never read the Bible, because it wasn't necessary for him. He said this church had been his god, his joy and his number one concern.

This man loved the church but never had a relationship with God. For more than 20 years he proved his undying love for the church without knowing God. The church became his object of worship. This man, although obviously a good man, was guilty of what

I call *Ecclesio-idolatry*, that is, the act of worshipping the church rather than God. Churches around the world are full of people who are just like this deacon, who love the church yet have no relationship with God.

We live in a generation where the masses have elevated some spiritual leaders to rock star status. Among the true worshippers who crowd into the houses of worship every week, there are those who are there not to worship God but to worship the spiritual leader. There are members of churches for whom their worship experience is incomplete if the pastor is absent from church worship. They come to church to encounter the leader whom they have elevated to god status. However, the divine obligation of the clergy is to constantly remind the congregants that they themselves are nothing more than sign posts, called to lead believers into deeper intimacy with God. High profile spiritual leaders like Bishop T. D. Jakes, Pastor of the Potter's House in Dallas, Texas; Bishop Eddie Long, Pastor of the New Birth Church in Atlanta, Georgia; Joel Olsten, Pastor of Lakewood Church in Houston, Texas, and a few others, recognize the status to which they have been elevated by some people and they are, therefore, very intentional in using their lofty status to point their congregants and followers toward a deeper spiritual reality beyond themselves.

The phenomenon of elevating clergy to god status is not new. The Apostles Paul and Barnabas dealt with this issue when they went to the city of Lystra to preach the gospel. While preaching at one their synagogues, Paul commanded a crippled man to stand to his feet. The crippled man got up and started walking around. When the people saw this, they elevated Paul and Barnabas to god status, saying of Paul and Barnabas, "The gods have become like men and have come down to us." They named Barnabas and Paul after their gods Zeus and Hermes, and brought bulls and flowers to offer sacrifices to the Apostles. When Paul found out about this he was so frustrated with them that he rent his clothes and asked, why are you doing this? We are just human beings attempting to point you to a deeper reality so that you might enjoy the intimacy that God has to offer (Acts 14:1-18 KJV). In our generation, too many clergy persons enjoy the god status to which they have been elevated. Thus, some worshippers never move beyond the clergy to experience real intimacy with God. John the Baptist had to remind his followers that he was not the Christ, because the Christ was preferred before him. He acknowledged that he had to decrease while Jesus increases (John 3:30KJV).

The Faith Challenge is designed to help the reader put these religious tools in the proper perspective so that they might be more effective at moving into deeper intimacy with God.

# Chapter 1

# Carnal *vs.* Spirit

A carnal-dominated life prevents us from moving into deeper intimacy with God and thus precludes us from walking in our divine destiny. It is possible to have a "surface relationship" with God as a carnal-dominated person, but one will never know the richness of deep divine intimacy until one makes the decision to "walk in the spirit" (Gal 5:16 KJV). Watchman Nee suggests, "There are two major decisions that every Christian must make. The first is the decision to convert from sin to salvation by grace. The second decision is to convert from carnal to spiritual by choice."

## The carnal nature

People refer to the carnal nature in many ways. It is often referred to as *ego,* or *self,* or even *flesh.* Whatever the name, it reflects the same reality. Deepak Chopra contends that the ego is actually a false self, pretending to be you. "The ego is your self-image; it is your mask; it is the role you are playing. Your social mask thrives on approval. It wants to control, and it is sustained by power, because it lives in fear."[1] The social psychologist Mark Leary was content to refer to the carnal nature as the *self;* as he points out, "The self is the main obstacle to spiritual advancement... because the constant stream of trivial concerns and egocentric thoughts keeps people locked in the material and profane world, unable to perceive sacredness, and divinity."[2] Even our Lord at times referred to the carnal nature as *the self.* He told His disciples, "If any man will come after me, let him deny *himself,* and take up his cross, and follow me" (Matthew 16:24KJV). The Apostle Paul teaches us that, "...to be carnally minded is death... Because the carnal is enmity against God: for it is not subject to the law of God, neither indeed can be. So then they that are the carnal cannot please God" (Romans 8:6-8 KJV). There is unanimous agreement between our Lord, spiritual teachers, psychologists, and the Holy Scriptures that the carnal nature represents everything that is wrong with us.

Life's most challenging struggle is with the carnal nature. This struggle is so challenging because the carnal has so cleverly woven itself into the inner fabric of our lives that it is difficult to recognize. Like a chameleon, the carnal nature blends perfectly into our personalities, so much so that we embrace it as if it is supposed

---

[1] Deepak Chopra, *The Seven Spiritual Laws of Success*. Pg. 17.

[2] Jonathan Haidt, *The Happiness Hypothesis*. Pg. 240.

to be there. The carnal nature has done such an extraordinary job at integrating into the human psyche that we have labeled manifestations of its presence as natural human tendencies that we tolerate in ourselves and others. Excessive anger, hatred, rage, greed, jealousy, insatiable wanting, superiority and inferiority complexes, etc., are traits that we well recognize but do not realize that they all emerge from the carnal nature. We agree that these, and other traits like these, are undesirable. We also agree that the world would be better off without them. Some people may attend anger management classes to help manage their anger and rage. Others may work very hard to get their jealousy under control through counseling or some other psychological rationalization. Most of us work hard to eliminate these unwanted traits from our lives. However, unless we acknowledge that these traits are manifestations of the dominance of the carnal nature, fighting these traits one by one is like swatting mosquitoes one by one, rather than cleaning up the swamp that breeds them. It is difficult, however, to convince people that there is a carnal nature and that they are living under its dominance.

The struggle with the carnal nature is so challenging, secondly, because even when its presence and dominance are brought to light, it has been with us for so long that it has convinced us that we can't live without it. We have identified so closely with the carnal nature that it is actually in control of our lives. It has seduced us into believing that it is us and we are it. It therefore controls everything in our lives from what we think, to whom we gravitate toward, to how we respond to life's circumstances, even to how we worship and pray.

The carnal nature is a living entity with intelligence, a goal, and a ferocious survival instinct. It is clever enough to allow a surface relationship with God and with others, but never a deep intimate relationship because intimacy poses a threat to its survival. Deep intimacy requires relating to each other on the basis of being, without the external roles, titles, masks or any other carnally created self images. Most relationships are merely an interfacing of roles. For example, a man plays many roles and interacts with others on the basis of the different roles. To his children he plays the role of father. To his wife he plays the role of husband. At his job he plays the role of boss or subordinate. But true intimacy occurs when he decides to relate to others simply on basis of being. True intimacy with God begins when I choose to be honest about who I am before Him. This is intimidating to the carnal nature because it relies on these superficial roles for its survival. Without these roles the carnal has no identity. Therefore, the carnal nature fights to keep all relationships on a superficial level, that is keep us relating on the basis of carnal created roles rather than on the basis of being. Richard Foster correctly asserts that, "Superficiality is the curse of our age… the desperate need today is not for a greater number of intelligent people, or gifted people, but for deep people…the spiritual life calls us to move beyond surface living into the depths."[3] Foster is quite

---

[3] Richard Foster, *Celebration of Discipline*. Pg. 30.

aware that when God created you, He created a masterpiece. There is so much more to you than you ever dreamed or imagined. There is a depth dimension to you that is so profound, that if you were to get in touch with it, it would transform your life. There is a depth dimension to every friendship, relationship, marriage, church, job and family that probably has not been explored; therefore, you miss the true blessings that they have to offer. When we deal with everything on a surface level, or from a superficial perspective, we miss the depth. If you carefully examine any major body of water you will find that regardless of what's happening on the surface of the water, whether it's peaceful and serene, or if it's blistering and chaotic, in the depths there is profound stillness. When you live on the surface you will always be beset by drama, chaos, and confusion, interrupted by brief moments of peace and serenity. However, if you can get off the surface and get to the depths, it wouldn't matter much what's happening on the surface, you could still have peace. Did you know that in the heart of a tornado there is profound stillness? It is the outer surface of that tornado that tears up property and destroys lives. Living on the surface, says Richard Foster, is the great problem of our generation.

The carnal nature does not resist surface relationships, especially with God, because it is cunning enough to know that this will appease you. The carnal nature is the great negotiator; it will make compromises with you. However, it will do everything in its power to stop you from moving into a deeper divine relationship. It will compromise by only mildly resisting your desire to attend church, if you are determined to do so, but it will vehemently defy any attempt to make a commitment to the church. It will allow you to enter the worship service, but it will sabotage your effort to engage in true worship. True worship is the ultimate spiritual activity and therefore provides a threat to the carnal nature. Jesus said, "But the hour cometh, and now is, when the true worshippers shall worship the Father in spirit and in truth: for the Father seeketh such to worship Him" (John 4:23KJV). The carnal nature will consent to your becoming associated with the church, but will provide compelling excuses for why you should not get involved in ministries that are designed to promote spiritual growth. Spiritual growth is simply becoming less carnal. The carnal nature will do anything to survive and accomplish its goal. The carnal nature will tolerate a "prayer life" as long as it controls the content of your prayers. God does not honor carnal prayers. Maybe that is the reason so many prayers go unanswered. James says, "The earnest prayer of a righteous person has great power and wonderful results" (James 5:16NLV). Prayers are powerful when they are offered by spiritual people or, as James puts it, *righteous* people. James also explains the precise reason some people do not get what they ask for in prayer: "What is causing the quarrels and fights among you? Isn't it the whole army of evil desires at war within you? You want what you don't have, so you scheme and kill to get it. You are jealous for what others have, and you can't possess it, so you fight and quarrel to take it away from them. And yet the reason you don't have what you want is that you don't ask God for it. And even when you do ask, you don't get it because your whole motive is wrong—you want only what will give you pleasure" (James 4:1-4NLV). This passage suggests that the carnal nature is able to dictate the content of our prayers. And when prayer is offered out of the carnal nature, it literally asks God to give it the very things that will strengthen it. That is why praying out of your carnal nature will always render your prayers ineffective.

During the early days of American history, in the gold rush era there was a married couple who wanted to get in on the gold bonanza. They had no luck in America so they decided to sell their house and move to Europe, where gold mines were being found everywhere. They were also very unsuccessful there. So they moved back to America and went back to their old home to try to talk the person into selling their home back to them. But when they arrived at their old home, the entire area was fenced off and scores and scores of excavators were working. They asked the men working there, "where is the owner of this property?" They answered, "He moved to Paris and bought a palace, his property sits on the biggest gold mine ever discovered in American history." The most valuable commodities you have are never on the surface of your life; like a gold mine, they are treasured deep within. Until you get off the surface and go deep within, you will never get in touch with them. Dorothy, in the Wizard of Oz, thought she had to go to a wizard to get what she wanted when she had what she needed with her all the time. The cowardly lion thought the wizard could give him courage. The scarecrow thought he needed someone beyond himself to give him intelligence. And the tin man thought he needed some external reality to give him the capacity to get in touch with his emotions. The four of them were all on the same journey, yet each of them already had what they were looking for within. They were so busy living on the surface that they missed what their inner realities had to offer. God has already given us what we need, but we will never find it living on the surface. It is buried deep within. Shakespeare says it best, "Our remedies oft in ourselves do lie."

People who live their lives on the surface are always looking for wizards. They are so desperate that they become gullible. They are perfect targets to be exploited and manipulated by charlatans. Often they will find a wizard, whether they call themselves prophetess, prophet, apostle, bishop, doctor, or Rev. Wizard. Sometimes they are counselors, family members, friends, coworkers, church members or even spouses, parents or children. Wizards come in all shapes and sizes. And all your wizards are going to do is make you get them something that only benefits them, but often puts you at risk. That's why the wizard told Dorothy and her friends to "go get the witch's broom before I help you." But if you pull back the curtain, you'll discover that the wizard is a spiritual midget trying to get you to ignore the little man behind the screen. Wizards so easily manipulate people who live on the surface. Superficiality is indeed the curse of our age. God needs people of depth. The church needs people of depth. The community, city, country, and the world need people of depth!

The struggle with the carnal nature is not a new phenomenon. Throughout scripture, individuals and communities have had to constantly contend with the carnal nature. The two most troubled congregations in scripture are the congregation of Israel under the leadership of Moses, and the congregation at Corinth under the leadership of Apostle Paul. Both of these congregations' trouble stemmed from their refusal to make the transition from living in the carnal to living in the spiritual. Even after 40 years of pastoral leadership and having witnessed the miracle of the Red Sea and numerous miraculous deeds perform by God through the hand of Moses, Moses still said of this carnal congregation, "For I know how rebellious and stubborn you are. Even now, while I am still with you, you have rebelled against the LORD" (Deuteronomy 31:27 NLT).

The Apostle Paul said of the Corinthian Christians, "And I, brethren, could not speak unto you as unto spiritual, but as unto carnal, even as unto babes in Christ. I have fed you with milk, and not with meat: for hitherto ye were not able to bear it, neither yet now are ye able. For ye are yet carnal: for whereas there is among you envying, and strife, and divisions, are ye not carnal, and walk as men?" (I Corinthians 3:1-3KJV). Both of these biblical congregations experienced a *surface* relationship with God but missed out on the opportunity to enjoy deep intimacy with God because of their decisions to remain carnal.

Jacob has to be considered one of the most carnal personalities in the Bible. However, the way Jacob turned out was not all his fault. He got his name, Jacob, which means trickster, supplanter or manipulator, from a situation over which he had no control. He was cursed with that name because of a situation that took place during his birth. He was the second born of twins. During the birth process, someone noticed that his hand grasped the heel of his older brother Esau. People interpreted that to mean that even at birth, Jacob desired his older brother's position so much that he would do anything to supplant him. The problem with this is that Jacob was only an infant and had not even come into the consciousness of his presence. Yet, he was labeled a trickster or supplanter on the basis of a situation over which he had no control or awareness. The adults in connection with the situation projected their negative opinions onto Jacob. He grew up in a community that expected him to be what they had named him, thus he became what they expected. He wasn't born a supplanter or trickster, but was shaped into what he had become by his community. Aristotelians argue that babies are born *tabula rasa*, which advances the notion that individuals are born without built-in mental content, and that their knowledge comes from experience and perception. Jacob's community shaped him into a man who had one of the most carnal personalities in the Bible.

In the 32nd chapter of the book of Genesis, Jacob came to a critical crossroads. He reached a dilemma in his life where that crucial decision that Watchman Nee talks about had to be made. He had to choose to embrace the Israel (spiritual) in him, or continue to live according to the Jacob (carnal) in him. Jacob's epic struggle at Peniel is one that anyone who wants to enjoy intimacy with God must engage. He had to decide whether to remain carnal and continue on his current path of trickery and deception, and miss his divine assignment, or to become spiritual and embrace his spiritual inheritance.

## The carnal nature is the portal for demonic access

The carnal is the portal through which the demonic accesses our lives. Psychologist Jonathan Haidt agrees that "the self is Satan's portal."[4] Saint Matthew's account of Jesus' temptation in the wilderness reveals that the devil's only point of access into our lives is through the carnal nature: "Then Jesus was led by the Spirit into the desert to be tempted by the devil. After fasting forty days and forty nights, he was hungry. The tempter came to him and said, 'If you are the Son of God, tell these stones to become bread.' Jesus answered, 'It is written: "Man does not live on bread alone, but on every word that comes from the mouth of God."' Then the devil took him to the holy city and had him stand on the highest point of the temple. 'If you are the Son of God,' he said, 'throw yourself down. For it is written: "He will command his angels concerning you, and they will lift you up in their hands, so that you will not strike your foot

---

[4] Haidt, Pg.239.

against a stone.'" Jesus answered him, 'It is also written: "Do not put the LORD your God to the test."' Again, the devil took him to a very high mountain and showed him all the kingdoms of the world and their splendor. 'All this I will give you,' he said, 'if you will bow down and worship me.' Jesus said to him, 'Away from me, Satan! For it is written: "Worship the LORD your God, and serve him only."' Then the devil left him, and angels came and attended him" (Matthew 4:1-11NIV). This passage reveals that the devil accesses our lives by entering through one of three carnal portals.

The first carnal portal is the appetite. When Jesus was hungry, the devil spoke to His appetite because he knew that was an available portal to enter into His life. Our appetite for food, drink, clothes, shelter, sex, and other basic human needs, if controlled by the carnal nature, would provide access to the demonic. When the demonic is allowed to dictate how we satisfy these basic needs, it will always lead to pain and destruction.

The second carnal portal is the need for negative attention or drama. The devil then took Jesus to the highest point of the temple and told Him to jump. The temple area is the most populated place in Jerusalem. There, Jesus would surely have an audience to witness this sensation. Had Jesus jumped, I'm convinced He would have destroyed Himself, but He would have gotten recognition and created the drama that the carnal nature so desperately craves. The carnal nature allows the devil to create scenarios that promise negative attention or drama so that it might be strengthened, even if causes destruction. The carnal nature is energized by negative attention, but ignores positive attention. I often counsel people who constantly talk about all that is negative and wrong in their lives, but never seem to see the positive or good in their lives. This is so because the carnal nature is empowered by negative energy. For example, I was counseling a young man who took one hour to tell me one long negative story. The next session, I decided to counter everything bad he had to say about his situation with something good or positive about it. After only 30 minutes of going back and forth with him from negative to positive, he became frustrated and stormed out of my office, accusing me of mocking him and making light of his situation by not taking him seriously. However, what actually happened was that his carnal nature was frustrated by its inability to nourish itself with a negative story. The carnal prefers to remember negative, painful experiences rather than pleasant, positive ones, because it loves drama.

The final carnal portal that provides demonic access is the desire for worldly success. The devil told Jesus, if you worship me I will give you worldly success. The devil is asking Jesus to trade His soul for fortune and fame. That is, abandon everything you know to be Godly, moral, and right, including your life's purpose, for worldly success. The media is filled with tragic stories of deeply carnal people who have committed the most dastardly deeds for worldly success. The carnal is a false self, created, sustained and empowered by obliviously embracing a satanic perception of reality. The carnal nature's dominance is what I call *continuously temporary,* because its dominance can be terminated at any moment but its reign can also last a lifetime. The carnal nature's most intimidating adversary is Spirit. Spirit has the power to annihilate the carnal at any time. The carnal nature is aware of its own volatility and, more importantly, of the eternal stability of Spirit. Spirit has always been here and will always be. Spirit is never threatened by anything, because nothing real can ever be intimidated. Spirit knows that in the end when the carnal has passed away, it will remain.

### How can we transcend the carnal nature?

So the question becomes, how do we transcend something that is so intricately woven into our very being? Paul infers in Romans Chapter 7 that the resolution to this issue is not the futile attempt to permanently transcend the carnal nature. That is, to overcome the carnal once and for all never having to be bother with it ever again. But to become aware of its reality, a witness to its presence, to be the watcher of its activities. He writes, "I know perfectly well that what I am doing is wrong, and my bad conscience shows that I agree that the law is good. But I can't help myself, because it is sin inside me that makes me do these evil things. I know I am rotten through and through so far as my old sinful nature is concerned. No matter which way I turn, I can't make myself do right. I want to, but I can't. When I want to do good, I don't. And when I try not to do wrong, I do it anyway. But if I am doing what I don't want to do, I am not really the one doing it; the sin within me is doing it. It seems to be a fact of life that when I want to do what is right, I inevitably do what is wrong. I love God's law with all my heart. But there is another law at work within me that is at war with my mind. This law wins the fight and makes me a slave to the sin that is still within me. Oh, what a miserable person I am! Who will free me from this life that is dominated by sin? Thank God! The answer is in Jesus Christ our Lord. So you see how it is: In my mind I really want to obey God's law, but because of my sinful nature I am a slave to sin" (Romans 7:16-25NLV). Paul makes us aware of his struggle with his carnal nature. He never really defeats the carnal nature in the sense of breaking free from it once and for all. For him, it was a constant struggle. His greater struggle, however, was that at one point he was unaware of what was going on with himself, for he says, "I don't understand myself at all" (Vs.15NLT). At First, Paul was unaware that it was the carnal nature wreaking havoc in his life. Paul's expression of his struggle is similar to a prowler who had been entering your home every night without your knowledge, and stealing valuable items and destroying your property. Every morning when you awaken, you would notice the missing items and damage, but would not be able to understand why or by whom your house was being damaged and looted. And then one night when the prowler was in your home, you turned on the lights and caught the prowler in the very act. He is now aware that you know of his presence. If the prowler decides to fight or flee, you at least now understand why your house is being damaged and looted and who's responsible for it, which is a victory in itself. It was only when Paul became aware of his carnal nature that he attained the upper hand. It was simply Paul's awareness of the carnal nature that holds it at bay. Paul's victory was also implied in the fact that he admitted "…I am doing what I don't want to do." The simple admission that he doesn't want to do the evil, suggests that he is aware that it is his carnal nature that desires it, and not his true authentic self. The fact that he doesn't want to do it is a victory, of sorts. I once knew a man who bragged about his "moral victories." When he made plans to satisfy his carnal nature and something came up to foil his plans, he counted it a victory over the carnal nature simply because he did not engage in the act. But true victory is more than not engaging in the carnal act because the opportunity didn't allow for it; rather, it is not wanting to engage in the act.

**The spiritual nature**

Spirit is so important because Spirit is essentially who we are. God formed man out of the dust and then breathed into him Divine Content. This breath is man's God essence, or Spirit. God preexisted creation therefore, Spirit existed before matter. Spiritually speaking, we were always a part of God and we always will be. When these bodies dissolve our Spiritual essence will *return* to God. The fact that we *return* to God upon bodily dissolution suggests that we were with God before we connected with our physical bodies. God told

Jeremiah, "I knew you before I formed you in your mother's womb" (Jeremiah 1:5NLV). The spiritual aspect of our being is eternal but the body is temporal. We are, therefore, primarily spiritual beings who have a temporary physical experience rather than physical beings who have occasional spiritual experiences. Deepak Chopra has suggested, "We (humans) are here to find out on our own that our true Self is spiritual, that essentially we are spiritual beings that have taken manifestation in physical form. We're not human beings (physical beings) that have occasional spiritual experiences — it's the other way around: we're spiritual beings that have occasional human (physical) experiences." [5] Since Spirit is essentially who we are, it makes sense to allow Spirit to play the lead role in our lives.

Everyone has the same amount of Spirit. There is not a person who has more God in him than others. We don't have varying degrees of the amount of God in us. Spirit is not given out in measurements. That is, Mr. Jones doesn't have 86% Spirit and Ms. Davis has 73% Spirit and the Reverend Smith has 97% Spirit. No, we all have the same amount of Spirit. There is not a person more "spiritual" than another in terms of having more Spirit quantitatively. However, human carnality does vary in degrees. There are those who are more or less carnal than others. The carnal nature, like chaff covering a wheat kernel, covers the spiritual nature. As the carnal nature becomes less and less prominent in our lives, the spiritual becomes more and more prominent. One of the miscalculations we

[5] Chopra, Pg. 82.

make when we are trying to "grow spiritually" is to think that we can somehow get more Spirit in us. But how could one be more of what he already is? The challenge for spiritual growth is not in becoming more spiritual, which is impossible, but in becoming less carnal, for the less carnal we become the more spiritual we become. When the carnal fades away there is nothing left but Spirit, your true authentic God content.

It is only through Spirit that intimacy with God can be enjoyed. The traditional spiritual disciplines such as prayer, meditation, worship, scripture reading, and others cannot be exercised effectively unless they are done through the Spirit. Prayer is powerless unless it is done in the Spirit (Romans 8:26). Worship is an empty exercise unless it is done in the Spirit (John 4:23). The scriptures cannot be fully understood without the Spirit (I Cor. 2:13). True love, joy, peace, patience, kindness, goodness, and faithfulness cannot be experienced or expressed without the Spirit (Gal. 5:22).

In the Spirit is where the truth of God resides and it is knowing His truth that makes us free (John 8:32). Free from what, you may ask? Free from the lies, falsehoods, and distortions created by the carnal nature which breeds fear and alienation. However, in the Spirit is where the peace of God is manifested. It is only when we lose awareness of His Presence that we become afraid.

## True love can only be found in Spirit

In the Spirit is where true love resides. The Greeks have at least three words that are equivalent to our English word love. *Eros* is a legitimate expression of love. Eros has sexual, erotic, or romantic connotations. However, inherent in eros is its polar opposite: hatred, fear and alienation. Surely you have heard countless stories of romantic couples who expressed eros love to each other in one instant and then expressed hatred and rage at one another the next. In extreme cases, one ends up physically attacking or killing the other. How could this be, you may ask? They appeared to be so in love. They probably were legitimately in love but it was eros, which contains its polar opposite and something will eventually trigger the opposite polarity at some point in the relationship.

Another word for love that the Greeks use is *philios*. This is the root word for Philadelphia. Philios' expression of love is brotherly love, which is where the city of Philadelphia gets its nickname. Philios is a legitimate expression of love. But just like eros, it too has an inherent polar opposite, which is often expressed in fear, hatred, jealousy, envy, competition and the like, against the person with whom you are in a philios love relationship. Life long friends become enemies. Family members who once loved one another become enemies over what seems to be the most trivial matters. If philios love is what holds the relationship together, something eventually will trigger the emergence of its polar opposite. Robert

Louis Stevenson reminded us that if one embraces Dr. Jekyll, one must also deal with Mr. Hyde. They come as a package deal, they are polar opposites.

But *agape* love is the highest form of love, because it has no opposite. It is complete within itself. It is pure love from top to bottom. I Corinthians 13 offers the greatest description of agape I have ever read. This kind of love can only be experienced and expressed in the Spirit. Agape love is so rare that when it is manifested it is almost impossible for most people to recognize it. It is often construed as weak or crazy. For example, a young man promised to marry a certain young lady after he finished graduate school. She waited three years for him to finish. While she waited for the man she loved to finish school, she passed up several quite impressive eligible bachelors, whom, were it not for her love and commitment to her grad school student, she would have surely dated. When he finally finished graduate school, with her financial assistance, he had a change of heart. He told her that he was no longer in love with her and desired to move on with his life. He argued that he deserved to be happy and that she didn't make him happy anymore. He apologized for holding up her life for more than three years and offered to reimburse her for the financial assistance she provided while he was a student. When he finished speaking, he braced himself for what he thought would surely be a whirlwind of anger, rage, and a flood of negative emotions, followed by a violent verbal attack punctuated with profanity, name calling, and damning his very soul to hell and perhaps even physical attack. However, she took him by the hand and looked into his eyes, with tears rolling down her cheeks, and said to him, "All I desire for you is to be happy, full of joy and at peace, and if I am the one who is blocking those wonderful energies from flowing into your life, I will step aside." He explained to me that he thought that was a strange response and concluded at least two things. The first is that she didn't love him either and wanted out of the relationship as much as he did. Or, that she was going to somehow, at some point, get even with him. He was literally baffled and didn't know what to make of her response. I had to explain to him that neither of his imaginary scenarios had to be true, but that perhaps he had had an encounter with true agape love and didn't even recognize it. Her love for him had no opposite. It was pure and undefiled. I also suggested that he might have made a big mistake by allowing such a rare human being to walk out of his life.

Miracles can only be wrought in the Spirit. Jesus' disciples were perplexed as to why they could not exorcise the demon out of a boy whose father had brought to them. After Jesus performed the exorcism, He explained to His disciples that "This kind does not go out except by prayer and fasting" (Matthew 17:21 KJV). Prayer and fasting are spiritual disciplines designed to move those who participate deeper into the spiritual realm. Jesus was the greatest miracle worker the world has ever seen, because Jesus is the ultimate Spiritual Man.

The Faith Challenge's goal is to bring us into the awareness of the existence of the carnal nature so that we might bring it under the subjection of the Spirit, thus, liberating us to move into intimacy with God.

## Chapter 2

# Practicing the Spiritual Disciplines

O ver the next 30 days, the Faith Challenge will require that you exercise several of the spiritual disciplines, including prayer, fasting, meditation, worship and scripture reading. The practice of these spiritual disciplines is not designed to turn you into some mystical spiritual guru, if that's not God's will for your life. They are only tools in the Master's hands to chip away the carnal nature, to give way to the flowering of your spiritual nature. The great artist Michelangelo Buonarroti stood before a crude, unfinished, giant block of marble and he alone saw beyond it a seventeen foot tall statue of King David. He believed it was his vocation to simply chip away excess marble to set the brilliant statue free. Like Michelangelo, our God sees beyond our carnality a spiritual masterpiece, and uses these spiritual disciplines as tools to liberate it from our carnality.

I do not want you to be intimidated by these spiritual disciplines. You might be tempted to say, "This is not for me at this time, I'm only a beginner. I need to grow a bit more before I'm ready." But Richard Foster, who wrote the signature book on the subject of spiritual discipline entitled *Celebration of Discipline*, admits, "I, too am a beginner, even and especially after a number of years of practicing..."[6] So all of you confessed beginners rest assured that you are not alone.

## Prayer

The Faith Challenge will demand exercising the discipline of prayer daily. Jesus requires that we regularly engage the practice of prayer. In fact, Jesus expects it. When He says to His disciples, "When you pray..." it implies that prayer is a divine expectaion. Prayer is simply communication with God. This is a simple definition, but it is a profound reality. The fact that we can actually communicate with the God of the Bible is mind-numbing! The God of creation in the book of Genesis and the God of Abraham, Isaac, and Jacob actually engages in communication with us. The God who manifested Himself in the person of Jesus Christ is the recipient of our prayers. Prayer is, therefore, an extremely important spiritual engagement. Prayer is more than simply speaking; it is total communion with God. Prayer encompasses the entire being, not just

---

[6] Foster, Pg. 32.

the intellectual faculties but also the spiritual and the appetitive, as some suggest. Foster says it best: "Prayer catapults us onto the frontier of the spiritual life. Of all the Spiritual Disciplines prayer is the most central because it ushers us into perpetual communion with the Father... Prayer is the central avenue God uses to transform us."[7]

Jesus was very faithful to His prayer life. He would often retreat for extended periods for prayer. In fact, even right now our Lord prays for us! "It is Christ that died, yea rather, that is risen again, who is even at the right hand of God, who also maketh intercession for us" (Romans 8:34KJV). Jesus encourages us always to pray. "Men ought always to pray, and not to faint" (Luke 18:1 KJV).

The story is told about a man who bought a parcel of land because he was convinced that a treasure chest was buried somewhere on the land. After the purchase he and his two sons began to dig at many of the possible places indicated on the treasure map. They dug for many months. The digging developed the muscles in their backs, legs, and arms. The digging made them much stronger, and physically healthier. After several months of digging, they finally found the treasure chest filled with gold. The father said to his sons, "not only did we get what we were digging for, but we got a lot stronger in the process!" That's the way prayer works; not only does Christ guarantee that we will receive what we ask for in prayer, but we also grow a lot stronger spiritually by practicing the discipline of prayer.

---

[7] Foster, Pg. 73.

**Fasting**

Fasting is the practice of abstaining from food for spiritual purposes. Richard Foster writes, "Fasting can bring breakthroughs in
the spiritual realm that will never happen in any other way."[8] Jesus
pointed out to His disciples that there are some things that will not
be accomplished without fasting and prayer. Throughout the Bible,
fasting has been a discipline for the people of faith. Moses, David,
Elijah, Esther, Daniel, Anna, Paul, and Jesus all fasted.

Fasting should be purposeful. Fasting should not be engaged just
for the sake of fasting. There should be meaning and purpose for
your fasting (Esther 4:16; Acts 9:9; Deut 9:9; I Kings 19:8).

Fasting is practical. That is, fasting is an expected practice for
Christians. It is not a command, but it is a divine expectation. God
expects us to fast (Matt 6:16). Jesus didn't say *if you fast,* He said
*when you fast,* which suggests that fasting was a regular practice
among Jesus' audience.

Fasting is powerful. Foster contends, "Once the primary purpose
of fasting is firmly fixed in our hearts, we are at liberty to understand
that there are also secondary purposes in fasting. More than any
other discipline, fasting reveals the things that control us. We cover
up what is inside us with food, but in fasting these things surface."[9]
Fasting is powerful because it keeps balance in our lives. Food often

---

[8] Foster, Pg. 113.
[9] Foster, Pg. 105.

dominates our thoughts. Fasting reminds us that it is God's power that sustains us.

## Meditation

Meditation is making conscious contact with God. There are plenty of scriptural references to our need to meditate. Genesis 22 makes it clear that Isaac would go out into the fields to meditate. Joshua 1 says "do not let the law depart from your mouth but meditate on it day and night." Psalm 48 says, "Within your temple, O God, we meditate on your unfailing love." There is a biblical precedence for meditation.

Meditation is listening to God's voice to provide direction and insight for your life. It is not asking God for anything, but it is listening to God. Someone might ask, how would I know it's God speaking? Jesus said my sheep know my voice. If you are His sheep, you'll know it.

### Meditation Period

We prepare for meditation by designating a specific time during the day to meditate. When something is important to us, we have specific time set aside for it. We set aside time for our appointments — doctor's, lawyer's, meeting, church, work, class. Everything in our lives that's important, we set aside time for it. You prove to God that you are taking Him seriously by allotting designated time every day to make conscious contact with Him. You need a specific time designed for meditation.

## Meditation Place

You will need a specific place for meditation. You will need a place that's pleasant to you, and free of negative vibes or energy. It should be quiet. No phones or television or radio, no interruptions.

## Meditation Posture

The Bible advocates a variety of positions for meditation, from lying prostrate on the floor to standing with hands lifted. David even talked about meditation while lying upon his bed. So the best posture is the one that's most comfortable to you. However, you should be in a position where there is no obstruction to the flow of energy through your body. That is, your legs or arms should not be crossed, and your back should be straight.

## Worship

Paul says, ""I beseech you therefore, brethren, by the mercies of God, that ye present your bodies a living sacrifice, holy, acceptable unto God, [which is] your reasonable worship. And be not conformed to this world but be transformed by the renewing of your mind that you may prove what the will of God is, that which is good and acceptable, or well pleasing and perfect to God which your reasonable worship"(Romans 12:1-2KJV).

In this passage, Paul educates the Christians in Rome regarding the true tenets of Christian worship. The Apostle calls their attention to the inspiration of worship. The greatest inspiration to worship should be "the mercies of God." God's mercies are everything He has given us that we don't deserve. He has given us salvation, love, joy, peace, The Holy Spirit, and so many other tangible and intangible commodities too numerous to name. To become aware that God has poured out all of these mercies on us, according to Paul, should inspire us to pour forth praise and thanksgiving—in other words, worship!

**Scripture reading**

Scripture is perhaps the most important means by which God speaks to us. Scriptural reading is designed to transform your life. There is a difference between studying the scripture and what Richard Foster calls devotional reading. "In study of the scripture, a high priority is placed upon interpretation: what it means. In devotional reading of scripture, a high priority is on application: what it means to me."[10] Daily reading of the scripture is tantamount to God

[10] Foster, Pg. 126.

giving us a daily dose of instruction, empowerment, encouragement, inspiration, and comfort. Who would want to miss out on that?

Our challenge for the next 30 days is to allow God to work on us with the tools identified in this chapter, to draw us into more profound intimacy with Him.

## How Does the Faith Challenge Work?

The Faith Challenge 30-day program will seem very demanding at first, because your carnal nature will strongly resist. Your carnal nature will manufacture a variety of excuses as to why you cannot begin "right now," or why you have to pause and take a break from it halfway through, or why you cannot or should not finish the program. Perhaps there will be times during the Faith Challenge when legitimate emergencies will arise and you will have to put the program aside for a day or two, or even a week or longer. However, I encourage you to resume the program as soon as possible, on the current day. You will have plenty of time to make up the part of the program you missed.

This book contains 30 daily assignments designed to deepen your intimacy with God, heighten your self-awareness, cleanse your spiritual field and put you in the position to have the desires of your heart to manifest in your life. The first eight days of the Faith Challenge, from Sunday to Sunday, are dedicated to purification.

There are daily exercises in the Faith Challenge to begin the inner purification process.

The next week, starting Monday and ending Sunday, is dedicated to consecration. The act of consecration is setting something aside and declaring it holy. During this week of consecration, the Faith Challenge will encourage you to consecrate all your personal relationships as holy, so they might be appreciated as spiritual practices. When an interpersonal relationship is entered into or transformed into a spiritual practice, the objective of that relationship is to promote spiritual growth.

The following week, from Monday to Sunday, is devoted to compassion. Compassion is love in action. You will be given daily tasks in expressing your love to others. You will spend seven days "doing unto others as you would have them do unto you."

The final week of the Faith Challenge, from Monday to Sunday, is committed to contribution. The Faith Challenge will require you to practice the grace of giving. By doing this you will be making meaningful tangible and intangible contributions to individuals and causes that, by your judgment, need them the most.

The Faith Challenge ends on a Monday. This is a day of celebration where you spend the day giving thanks and demonstrating gratitude for everything that God has blessed you with.

The Faith Challenge program offers a 10 minute meditation instructional CD for your daily meditations. If meditation is a new discipline for you or if you just need additional help with meditation, as most of us do, this CD will guide you through your 10 minute daily meditations. Also, the Faith Challenge program offers 30 reminder bracelets. Each day of the Faith Challenge the program has a different challenge. During the course of our busy days we may sometimes forget what is today's particular challenge. The Reminder Bracelets has written on them the challenge for that particular day.

## Preparing for the Faith Challenge

The Faith Challenge is designed to begin on Sunday with worship. Each daily task in the Faith Challenge is meant to be executed on the particular day suggested by the Faith Challenge Program. For example, day 2 of the Faith Challenge purposely falls on a Monday, day 3 purposely falls on Tuesday, and so on. In order for the Faith Challenge to be a blessing to your life, you should perform the prescribed task on the suggested day.

On Monday day 16 of the Faith Challenge, you will be required to spend one hour in a nursing home reading the scripture and interacting with the residents. You will need to identify a nursing home facility and call a couple of weeks in advance to inform the facility that you want to volunteer on that day. Some nursing homes require a police background check and other stipulations before they grant you access to their residents.

On Wednesday day 18, the Faith Challenge requires that you take food to a local food pantry. You will need to identify a food pantry and find out what the requirements are to deliver food. Find out what kinds of foods the pantry accepts, and what is the pantry's greatest need. If you do not wish to give food to a pantry because you want to be more personal with this task, the Faith Challenge allows you to grocery shop for a family in need. You should prayerfully identify the family that you are going to bless with groceries days before, so on that day you will not have to try to figure it out at the last minute. You also have 18 days to save as much money as you can for this task.

On Thursday day 19, the Faith Challenge calls for you to visit someone incarcerated. You should call the jail or juvenile center that's closest to you and find out what their visitation policies are. You may not know anyone incarcerated, but there is someone who needs a visit from you.

On Saturday day 21, the Faith Challenge encourages you to visit a homeless shelter. You should contact a local homeless shelter and inform the staff of your intention to visit. Find out the requirements for visitation, and make the adjustments so that you may be allowed to visit.

On Tuesday day 24, the Faith Challenge requires you to serve at your church. Call your church and inform the staff that at some point on that day you want to come in and serve in a ministry. Ask someone in charge to identify a need, and how may you serve on this day. If your church has no needs for you meet, call another church in your community and inform them of your intentions.

On Friday day 27, the Faith Challenge demands that for one year you offer your special talent, whether it's computer, accounting, legal services, janitorial services, or just serving as a resource person to be used in any area.

**Keeping a record**

The Faith Challenge program has provided space for you to write about your journey through the Faith Challenge. Journaling is an extremely important practice in the Faith Challenge, because journaling awakens your awareness to certain realities about yourself. Journaling causes you to pay close attention to your actions, which can bring you into the awareness of why you do some of the things you do. Journaling also provides you the freedom to express your thoughts and feelings. Journaling is a form of self-monitoring which is a necessary element for spiritual growth. Take the opportunity to journal at the end of each day during the Faith Challenge on the pages provided in the book.

# Chapter 3

# A Week of Purification
## Week 1: The week of purification

P urification is an extremely important function in every area of life. Health experts remind us of the necessity of maintaining a regular practice of purifying the body. We are encouraged to drink plenty of water to flush the body of toxins and harmful pollutants that may break down the immune system and leave it susceptible to disease. Saunas are also advised for bodily purification. Saunas are designed to induce profuse perspiration, which eliminates contaminants from the body. Colon cleansing, liver cleansing, and blood detoxification methods are all recommended to keep the body healthy.

The scientific community constantly points out the damage we are causing the planet by the continual release of poisonous waste in the air and waterways. Bottled water is one of the top-selling products around the world because it promises purified drinking water.

Fortune 500 companies are cashing in on our desire for purification, and are reaping record profits by peddling water, air, and environmental purification systems.

External purification is very important and must be taken seriously. However, inner purification, or internal cleansing, is even more important. In fact, the external pollution of the body and environment are extensions of the inner pollution that the human race continues to ignore. Man is the cause of all pollution, whether it is bodily or environmental.

Inner pollution prevents us from moving into deeper intimacy with God. It is for this reason the Scripture says, "But now you must get rid of all these things: anger, passion, and hateful feelings. No insults or obscene talk must ever come from your lips" (Colossians 3:8 GNT). It is impossible to enjoy full fellowship with God and receive the benefit of His peace if we are filled with inner pollution. Jesus said, "Happy are the pure in heart; they will see God!" (Matthew 5:8 GNT). That is to say, it is only when we rid ourselves of all inner pollution that we will be able to see God in any and all situations, which erases fear and dread and ushers us into a state of happiness.

Several years ago I traveled to Cuernavaca, Mexico for a month to study the Spanish language. We rented a beautiful house for a month. The estate was surrounded by an impressive stone wall. It had an outdoor heated pool, marble floors, perfect landscaping, and interesting masterpiece paintings on the walls. It was exquisite! I did not immediately notice how beautiful the house was, because I was distracted by a horrible stench in the air. It was impossible to rest or settle down until I found the source of the stench. I searched the entire house until I found that the odor was coming from the refrigerator. I opened the refrigerator door and found old molded cheese, rotten eggs, spoiled milk, and decaying fruit and vegetables. The refrigerator was also full of other stuff that was so decomposed I couldn't figure out what it was. I didn't want to wait for the woman from whom I rented the house to come and clean it; the smell was so bad, I decided to take care of it myself. After an hour of disposing of everything in the refrigerator and cleaning and disinfecting and deodorizing the refrigerator, it was "purified" and the stench had dissipated. No longer distracted by the stench, I was then able to appreciate the beauty of my surroundings. We are often surrounded by beauty; beauty in our relationships, beauty in our marriages, beauty in our jobs, and churches but often fail to appreciate the beauty because of our inner pollution. The Apostle Paul may have had this notion in mind when he wrote to Titus, "To the pure, all things are pure, but to those who are corrupted and do not believe, nothing is pure." (Titus 1:15NIV).

The principle for purification is the same for every area of life. For example, with bodily purification, we must not put anything in our bodies that will not help them attain and maintain maximum health. In addition, we must drink plenty of water to flush out any toxins that may have entered our bodies. The same is true with inner purification. I am learning not to allow anything into my spiritual field that I don't believe will enhance my relationship with God. I intentionally avoid situations and encounters that may make me feel bad or disturb my spirit. For example, certain kinds of music, movies, talk radio programs, news broadcasts, and some printed media I intentionally avoid because they may burden my spirit. Engaging in gossiping, judging, and criticizing seems like the right thing to do while you are doing it, but if you are sensitive to your spiritual state you'll notice a heaviness of spirit after engaging in such activities. Therefore, I purposely avoid that kind of behavior. J. A. Byers writes, "The justified believer must meet the conditions of complete separation and exclusive dedication of himself to God, in the sense that no guilty sinner can do. This is the believer's part. He must purify himself."[11] John says, "Every man that hath this hope in Him purifieth himself even as he is pure" (1 John 3:3KJV). "Having therefore these promises dearly beloved, let us cleanse ourselves from all filthiness of flesh and spirit, perfecting holiness in the fear of God" (II Corinthians 7:1KJV). J. A. Byers' commentary on this passage is important: "This brings the believer into the condition where God can fulfill His part. He can now take exclusive posses-sion of the dedicated temple, and sanctify it."[12] Apostle Paul asserts,

---

[11] J. A. Byers, *Sanctification*. Pg. 5.

[12] Byers, Pg. 5.

"And the very God of peace sanctify you wholly" (I Thessalonians 5:23KJV). "If a man purge himself from these, he shall be a vessel unto honour, sanctified, and meet for the Master's use, and prepared unto every good work" (II Timothy 2:21 KJV).

It is sometimes difficult to know how toxic we are until we have participated in a detoxification program. We carry around so much pain and animosity. For many of us, it is difficult to let go of evils that others have perpetrated against us. We carry in our conscious-ness the disappointments, failures, mistakes, and sins we have expe-rienced in the past. The accumulation of these negative experiences will poison our inner being if not properly managed. The toxicity of our spirits may manifest in our attitudes, thinking, conversations, and personalities. Regular inner purification is absolutely necessary.

Sanctification and purification have been mistakenly used syn-onymously. The two are very different. Sanctification in the tradi-tional biblical sense comes from the Greek word *hagiazo*, which literally means to be separated or to be "set apart." In the Bible, sanctification generally relates to a sovereign act of God whereby He "sets apart" a person, place, or thing through which His purpose may be accomplished. In the book of Exodus, God sanctifies a place of worship. "And there I will meet with the children of Israel, and the tabernacle shall be sanctified by My glory" (Exodus 29:43KJV).

Similarly, when a person is sanctified, he is being set apart by God for a specific divine purpose. The very moment we are saved in Christ we are sanctified and begin the process of being conformed to the image of Christ. As God's children, we are set apart from that moment to carry out His divine purpose. Saturday is typically my laundry day. I wash my clothes, iron, fold, and put them in their proper storage spaces so that when I am ready to wear them they are clean and available. Likewise, Sanctification is being cleansed by the blood of Christ and set apart to be used by God.

Purification, on the other hand, occurs when the sanctified is empowered through sanctification to take actions to purify himself. Sanctification is the action that God takes on us, and purification is the action that we take upon ourselves.

# Sunday Day 1
# A Day of Worship

*"True worshipers will worship the Father in spirit and in truth. The Father is looking for anyone who will worship him that way."* (John 4:23 KJV)

**Today's Challenge:** To worship God in spirit and in truth.

This is the first day of our Faith Challenge. It is appropriate to begin the Faith Challenge with "true worship." William Temple, the Archbishop of York says, "To worship is to quicken the conscience by the holiness of God, to feed the mind with the truth of God, to purge the imagination by the beauty of God, to open the heart to the love of God, to devote the will to the purpose of God." Richard Foster contends, "To worship is to experience Reality, to touch Life. It is to know, to feel, to experience the resurrected Christ in the midst of the gathered community. It is a breaking into the Shekinah of God, or better yet, being invaded by the Shekinah of God."[13]

Worship as a corporate spiritual discipline is extremely intimidating to the carnal nature. True worship cannot take place as long as the worshipper is encapsulated in the carnal. The carnal nature cannot help but call all of the attention to itself. The spiritual nature, on the other hand, in worship turns all of the attention toward God.

---

[13] Foster, Pg. 255.

That is, when one is worshiping in the carnal, one knows it because everything that happens in worship will always be about "me." This carnally created *Malady of Me-ism* caused Dr. Wayne Dyer to raise the question, "Can you imagine living one complete day without thinking about yourself? Nothing offending you, nothing disturbing you, nothing causing you to be angry?"[14] The answer is a resounding yes, especially when you become aware of the role of the carnal nature.

Now that we are aware of the carnal nature's intentions to sabotage our efforts to break free of its stronghold on our lives through exercising of the spiritual disciplines, we place ourselves in the position to become the *watcher* of its activities. Keep a close eye on the carnal during worship because the old saying is true, "*A watched pot never boils over.*"

Worship today, not as a spectator but as a participant. Engage fully in the service. Follow the worship leader's instructions carefully and submit yourself. Don't resist, surrender to the flow of the worship as directed by the worship leader. Rick Warren reminds us that "Surrendering to God is the heart of worship. It is the natural response to God's amazing love and mercy. We give ourselves to Him, not out of fear or duty, but in love."[15]

In worship today, allow the songs to speak directly to you. Let the scripture lesson apply to you. Let the sermon speak to you.

---

[14] Dr. Wayne Dyer, *Your Sacred Self.* Pg. 42.

[15] Rick Warren, *The Purpose Driven Life.* Pg. 80.

Allow yourself to literally become absorbed in the worship. Pray for yourself that God will manifest Himself to you during this 30 day Faith Challenge and draw you closer to Him to experience divine intimacy.

---

**The Faith Challenge Day 1**

➤ 20-minute daily devotion
  1. Scripture reading: Psalm 104
  2. Prayer: pray that the Lord would prepare your heart for worship.
  3. Meditation: 10-minute quiet meditation. Clear your mind and focus on your breathing.

---

# At the End of Day 1

On a scale from 1 to 10, 1 being hardly engaged and 10 being totally engaged, how engaged were you in worship today?

How did your carnal nature try to disrupt your worship today?

Write your personal reflections on the first day of the Faith Challenge.

## Monday Day 2

*"...Forgive anyone you are holding a grudge against."*

(Mark 11:25NLT)

**Today's Challenge**: Today I must forgive everyone from my past, including myself.

The inability to forgive is the main obstacle to deep intimacy with God. No doubt, you have evil perpetrated against you. The carnal nature will attempt to hold on to the offenses committed against you because it needs drama to help it to feel alive. The carnal nature feeds on grudges, pain, negative conflict, etc., to strengthen itself. The stronger the carnal nature becomes, the more profound will be our disconnect from God. Peter asked Jesus, "How many times must we forgive our brother, seven times?" Jesus said, "Until seventy times seven" (Matthew 18:21-22 KJV). Here, Matthew uses the Greek word, *hebdomēkontakis* which literally means countless times. Jesus wanted His disciples to be aware that holding grievances through an unforgiving heart hinders their ability to enjoy deeper intimacy with God. Jesus recognized that the carnal tendency to hold on to anger associated with being wronged by others, and the desire to seek revenge, not only disrupts our relationship with God but also robs us of our divine destiny.

The manner in which Jesus managed the crucifixion is a practical demonstration of the power of forgiveness. After Jesus had been abused, nailed to the cross, and lifted up, the first thing He said from the cross was, "Father, forgive them..." Jesus understood that if He were to finish the work of redemption and salvation, He had to begin with forgiveness. Forgiveness is so important that Jesus exercised this prerogative while in excruciating pain and in the presence of His perpetrators. He forgave those who crucified Him without their asking for it. In fact, He forgave even while they mocked and scorned Him because He was aware that forgiveness is not about trying to get back into the good graces of the perpetrator, but forgiveness is about being set free to fulfill our divine destiny. With all the power Jesus had at His disposal, He could have saved Himself from the cross and destroyed those who caused Him pain, but the work of salvation would never have been completed. Non-forgiveness would have ruined the divine plan. Non-forgiveness always ruins what God has in store for us. I often ask myself what wonderful things I have missed because of my unwillingness to forgive.

One of my close relative's life had stalled for many years. Nothing he did succeeded. His goals and aspiration never came to fruition, no matter how hard he worked. It was not until he went on a solo retreat and spent uninterrupted time with God that he discovered he had an anger problem. He had been holding a grudge against the circumstances of his upbringing. He was intensely resentful of the daily poverty, substance abuse, domestic violence, and dysfunction to which he had been subjected during his childhood. He knew his upbringing didn't have to be the way it was. He was aware that his plight was the result of a lifetime of bad decisions by his father. He approached life with resentment and anger. He therefore pursued his life's goals and ambitions, not with joy, optimism and freedom, but with grim determination, antipathy, and bitterness. He had created a spiritual atmosphere so toxic that nothing in his life could grow and prosper. All of his dreams and goals were stillborn; they never had a chance to prosper because the environment into which they were born was too poisonous for them to survive.

He had to learn the necessity of forgiveness of not only people, but also of life's situations. In order to purify his spiritual space and to make it fertile so that his plans might prosper, he had to exercise the power of forgiveness. He soon forgave the depressing life situation of his upbringing. He forgave the substance abuse, the poverty, the domestic violence and the dysfunction, and the people responsible for it. He literally went on a healthy forgiving spree! He forgave the socioeconomic system that created a culture that made it difficult for certain people to thrive. He forgave the drug trade and the so-called war on drugs. He forgave the ignorance and the insensitivity that created the conditions of his upbringing. He literally manufactured an exhaustive list of people and situations he needed to forgive.

He is now free. His entire demeanor has changed. His conversation is no longer the same. He pursues his goals with joy and love.

His life-long goals and desires seem to manifest effortlessly. He has an obvious peace and tranquility I had never seen in him, and it was because of the power of forgiveness.

One of the most difficult things for many people is to forgive self. Too many people choose to live in constant guilt. Living with a guilt-ridden conscience hinders our ability to enjoy deep intimacy with God. The Lord made provision for forgiveness so that guilt wouldn't keep us from divine intimacy. "If we confess our sins, he is faithful and just to forgive us [our] sins, and to cleanse us from all unrighteousness" (I John 1:9KJV). "Who being the brightness of [his] glory, and the express image of his person, and upholding all things by the word of his power, when he had by himself purged our sins, sat down on the right hand of the Majesty on high" (Hebrews 1:3KJV). "In whom (Jesus) we have redemption through his blood, [even] the forgiveness of sins" (Colossians 1:14KJV).

God has forgiven our sins, there is no more need for guilt. Our guilt arises from our inability to live in the present. When you spend too much time rehearsing the past it has the power to keep you entrenched in guilt, even though you have been forgiven by God.

**The Faith Challenge Day 2**

➢ 20-minute daily devotion
   1. Scripture reading: Matthew 18:21-35
   2. Prayer: pray for the power to forgive others and yourself.
   3. Meditation: 10-minute quiet meditation. Clear your mind and focus on your breathing.
➢ Food fast from 8:00am to 8:00pm
➢ In an effort to purify your thinking today, you should abstain from the internet, television, radio, and any other form of electronic entertainment, unless of course it is required for your job.
➢ Also, with fasting today you must pray at least four times: 9:00am, 12:00pm, 3:00pm and 6:00pm. Your prayer should include asking God to help you forgive specific people who have wronged you, and that your anger towards them might be transmuted to love.

## At the End of Day 2

List every person you forgave today and their offense against you.

Was there someone you had trouble forgiving? If so, why?

Of what did you forgive yourself?

Write your personal reflection on the second day of the Faith Challenge.

# Tuesday Day 3

*"And this is the blessing, wherewith Moses the man of God blessed the children..."* (Deut. 33:1 KJV)

**Today's Challenge:** Today I will bless everyone, everything, every situation, and every event for the entire day.

Did you know that God has endowed you with the power to bestow blessings? The first time the word *bless* is used in the Bible is in Genesis 1:22 when God blessed the man and the woman and told them to be fruitful and multiply. The Hebrew word for blessing in this passage is *barak*. In Deuteronomy 33:1, when Moses blessed the Children of Israel the same Hebrew word *barak* is used. This implies that not only does God possess the power to *barak* or to bless, but we too possess that same power to *barak* or to bless.

The power to bless is a God-given gift that far too many of us don't even realize we possess. "To bless means to wish, unconditionally and from the deepest chamber of your heart, unrestricted good for others and events. It means to hallow, to hold in reverence, to behold with awe that which is always a gift from God. He who is hallowed by your blessing is set aside, consecrated, holy, whole. To bless is to invoke divine care upon, to speak or think gratefully for, to confer happiness upon..."[16]

---

[16] Pierre Pradervand, *The Gentle Art of Blessing*. Pg. 149.

To bless people even though they may curse you; to bless situations even though they may seem to be against you; to bless events even if they are bothersome to you; defuses the circumstance of negative energy. Negative energy is always "disempowering" and counter-productive. Cursing those who curse you; and damning the situation that seems to be against you; and condemning the event that is bothersome to you; only charges the situation with more negative energy; this makes matters far worse.

A young pastor for whom I am mentor became extremely frustrated with his congregation. He often complained to me about the apathy and boredom that seemed to have taken over the congregation. This frustrated him to the point that he would scold and denounce the congregation for their apathy from the pulpit during Sunday morning worship. I counseled him that his angry ranting from the pulpit only infused an already-negative situation with more negative energy. It was like pouring gasoline on fire. I urged him that it is impossible to get positive change out of a congregation by being negative, so rather than scolding and condemning, I advised him to try loving and blessing and celebrating the things that the congregation did well.

Your coworker or boss who has always been annoying to you, today rather than resisting, embrace him and send him love from your heart and bless him with every good thing that comes to mind. The job that you dread going to, today just stop and thank God for the job and send that work place your love and blessing. If you are unemployed because of an economic situation beyond your control, don't curse the economy or the people you hold responsible for creating economic. Forgive the economy and send it your blessing and love. Today, bless your household and everything in it. Send it your love and grace.

Today, begin the process of dousing the flames of negativity with positive energy generated by your love and blessing.

---

**The Faith Challenge Day 3**

➤ A 20-minute daily devotion
1. Scripture reading: Psalm 34
2. Prayer: your prayer should include blessing everything, everyone, and every situation and circumstance that the Holy Spirit brings to mind while you are in prayer.
3. A 10-minute meditation: clear your mind and focus on your breathing.

➤ Today's prayer periods: 9:00am, 12:00pm, 3:00pm and 6:00pm. Your prayers should include bestowing blessings on particular people and situations.

➤ If tonight is your church's mid-week worship night, you are to attend.

---

# At the End of Day 3

Whom did you bless today?

What situation did you bless today? Explain.

Were there any situations today that you refused to bless? If so, why?

How did blessing everything make you feel?

Write your personal reflections on the third day of the Faith Challenge.

# Wednesday Day 4

*"Therefore judge nothing before the appointed time; wait
till the Lord comes."* (I Cor. 4:5NIV)

**Today's Challenge:** Today I will refrain from judging anyone or
anything.

Yesterday you spent the entire day blessing God, people, places
and situations. Today you will not judge anything or anyone. You
will find that it is literally impossible to bless and judge at the same
time. Blessing is the opposite of judging. Blessing is empowering,
but judging is disempowering. The act of blessing brings us into
deeper intimacy with God. The act of judging distances us from
God. The act of judging is the carnal nature's way of making one feel
superior to others. To feel superior to others makes it impossible for
one to relate to others in genuine and authentic ways. The manner in
which one relates to others is a reflection of one's relationship with
God. James says, "How can you say you love God whom you have
not seen but hate your brother whom you see every day?"

The act of judging is the condemnation of what is, and an arro-
gant desire to rearrange things the way you think they should be. It
infers that you, and you alone, know how things should be; that is
insanity. Judging is purely an act of the carnal nature. In the book,
*A Course in Miracles,* Dr. Helen Schucman states, "You have been

urged to refrain from judging, not because it is a right to be with-held from you. You cannot judge. You merely can believe the ego's (or carnal nature's) judgments, all of which are false."[17] Anything done out of the carnal nature is insanity. Jonathan Haidt asserts, "Judgmentalism is indeed a disease of the mind: it leads to anger, torment and conflict."[18] The Apostle Paul argues that all judging should cease, even judging oneself.

People who are engaged in the habit of judging are obviously most miserable. Chopra suggests that "Judgment is the constant evaluation of things as right or wrong, good or bad. When you are constantly evaluating, classifying, labeling, analyzing, you create a lot of turbulence in your internal dialogue."[19]

Today, don't judge but allow things to be as they are. Frederick Pearls once wrote, "I do my thing and you do yours. I am not in this world to live up to your expectations, and you are not in this world to live up to mine. You are you and I am I, and if by chance we find each other, then it is beautiful. If not, it can't be helped."

[17]  Dr. Helen Schucman, *A Course In Miracles*.
[18]  Haidt, Pg. 102.
[19]  Chopra, Pg. 21.

---

**The Faith Challenge Day 4**

➤ A 20-minute daily devotion

1. Scripture reading: Luke 6:27-37
2. Prayer: your prayer should include beseeching God's power to keep you from judging.
3. A 10-minute meditation: clear your mind and focus on your breathing.

➤ Prayer periods: 9:00am, 12:00pm, 3:00pm and 6:00pm. Your prayers should include invoking the Lord's power to keep you from judging.

➤ If tonight is your church's mid-week worship night, you are to attend.

# At the End of Day 4

Were you successful at not judging anything today? If not, what did you judge and why?

If you were successful at not judging today, describe how not judging made you feel.

Write your personal reflection for the fourth day of the Faith Challenge.

# Thursday Day 5

*"In everything you do, stay away from complaining..."*
(Philippians 2:14 KJV)

**Today's Challenge:** Today I refuse to complain about anything.

Complaining is another ploy of the carnal nature to mask your own inadequacies and faults. To complain is to take the focus off you and place it on someone, something, or some situation. Wayne Dyers writes, "Generally speaking, when you resort to complaining you employ an excuse of one kind or another, placing the responsibility for what's upsetting you on something or someone external to yourself... complaining about the way somebody performed is another way of making an excuse for why you're dissatisfied or unhappy." Complaining robs you of the opportunity for serious introspection without which there can be no personal maturity.

Complaining is the act of resisting present realities. To resist the present reality obviously means, at least to the person resisting, that the situation is negative. Complaining is an intensely negative action. When you complain about any negative situation you might be in, you are only adding more negative energy to the already-negative situation. That's why Jesus instructs us to "Bless those who curse you..." Blessing a curse offsets the negative energy that curses create.

Complaining is the carnal nature's way of attempting to convince you that you are superior to the person, thing, or circumstance you are complaining about. Complaining implies you are right and what you are complaining about is wrong. Complaining puts you at odds with what you are complaining about. Through complaining you make an enemy of the situation, and when the situation becomes your enemy it fights back and creates tension in your life. James said, "Do not complain against one another, my friend, so that God will not judge you" (James 5:9GN). Complaining puts us under the judgment of God.

---

**The Faith Challenge Day 5**

➢ A 20-minute daily devotion
  1. Scripture reading: Philippians 2:13-17
  2. Prayer: your prayer should include thanking God for all of the blessings that He has given you.
  3. A 10-minute meditation: clear your mind and focus on your breathing.

➢ Prayer periods: 9:00am, 12:00pm, 3:00pm and 6:00pm. Your prayers should be prayers of praise and thanksgiving.

➢ If tonight is your church's mid-week worship night, you are to attend.

---

## At the End of Day 5

Were you successful at not complaining today? If not, what did you complain about and why did you feel the need to complain?

If you did not complain today, how did you feel going through an entire day without complaining?

Do think you can make not complaining a permanent part of your lifestyle? If not, why?

Write your personal reflection on the fifth day of the Faith Challenge.

## Friday Day 6

*"There is now no condemnation for those who are in Christ Jesus."* (Romans 8:1 KJV)

**Today's Challenge**: Today, moment by moment, I will live in the Now.

The reason there is no condemnation for those who are in Christ, as Apostle Paul suggests, is the grace of God is offered moment by moment or in the Now. Grace and condemnation are mutually exclusive. They cannot occupy space at the same time. When grace enters, condemnation has to exit. Along with condemnation come fear, anxiety, aloneness, and sometimes anger, rage, and the feeling of worthlessness. On the other hand, along with grace come love, peace, wholeness, and the feeling of acceptance and worth. The word condemnation in Romans 8:1 is the Greek word *katakrima,* which suggests being damned to eternal separation from God. The very thought of living in deep intimacy with God is impossible if one is living under *katakrima.*

Paul puts it aptly, "Now no condemnation..." If there is no condemnation it means grace must be present. Implied here is that God's grace can only be experienced in the Now. God offers His grace in the present moment. Unless we can stay in the present moment we miss the full benefit of grace. Not only does grace save us from sin but it also creates an atmosphere of love, peace and wholeness. You may be a recipient of grace and experience forgiveness of sin but miss partaking of the atmosphere created by grace. We feel condemned when we live in the past, or when we project ourselves into the future. All your anger, rage, and pain are in your past experience. All your stress, fear, and anxiety are in your imagined future. Many people are living in constant anger or in constant fear. Most of us swing between the two. In one moment we are angry and upset over what has happened to us in the past, and in the next moment we are anxious and stressed over what might happen in the future. Very seldom do we recognize that grace abounds in the present moment. The presence of God can only be experienced in the present. You cannot experience His presence living in the past or projecting yourself into the future. His presence is present. My advice for you today is: Leave the past behind and come back from the future.

---

**The Faith Challenge Day 6**
➢ A 20-minute daily devotion
  1 Scripture reading: Matthew 6:25-34
  2 Prayer: your prayer should include beseeching God's power to keep you out of the past and future and remaining in the present.
  3 A 10-minute meditation: clear your mind and focus on your breathing.
➢ Prayer periods: 9:00am, 12:00pm, 3:00pm and 6:00pm. Your prayers should involve talking to God about what is happening in your life in that particular moment.

## At the End of Day 6

Living in the present moment can be difficult at first because we are so used to living in the past or projecting ourselves into the future. Did you find yourself constantly thinking of the past or the future? If so, what were those thoughts?

When you found yourself thinking about the past or projecting into the future, how did you bring yourself back into the present moment?

Did you find peace in the present moment? Explain.

Write your reflections about your experience of day 6.

## Saturday Day 7

*"If you listen carefully to the voice of the LORD your God*
*and do what is right in his eyes…. I will not bring on you*
*any of the diseases I brought on the Egyptians."*
(Exodus 15:26NIV)

**Today's Challenge:** Today I will listen intently for the voice of God in every situation.

There is never a time when God is not speaking. However, only those who are intentionally listening for His voice are able to hear it. This reality is demonstrated in the 6th chapter of the Gospel according to John: "'Father, bring glory to your name!' Then a voice spoke from heaven, 'I have brought glory to it, and I will do so again.' The crowd standing there heard the voice, and some of them said it was thunder, while others said, 'An angel spoke to him!'" (John 6:28-30 GNV). There were two factions in the crowd. One faction was not spiritually alert enough to recognize the Voice from heaven, thus they said it was merely thunder. The other faction was spiritually sensitive enough to recognize the Voice of the Spirit.

There is a spiritual message in every physical reality. If you are spiritually alert you will hear His voice in every situation. Several years ago I had been in a meeting with our church finance team. There were several projects that our ministry wanted to conduct.

These projects were very costly, but extremely beneficial for our church and the immediate neighborhood. My finance team gave me the disappointing news that not only could we not afford to do the project, but we also needed to cut other programs that our church was very fond of. I left the meeting very disappointed, almost depressed. As I drove home, I was listening to the gospel music station on the radio when a song by Dewayne Woods started playing entitled, "Let Go and Let God." There is a stanza in that song that says, "There is so much going on. Sometimes I can't find my way. And often times I struggle; struggle from day to day. I have to realize that it is not my battle; it's not my fight. I have to know if I put it in His hands that everything will be all right. Let go, and let God." Upon hearing those words I knew that God was speaking directly to me. When I received that stanza as the actual voice of God, I immediately cheered up. My disappointment and near depression dissipated at once. His voice brought me peace, right away! But it was only because I was in the spiritual position to hear His voice.

A married couple in our church was having marital problems and made an appointment with me for counseling. When the couple finally arrived at my office, they appeared to be too happy and giddy to be a couple in danger of losing their marriage. Before we entered my office the wife said, "We no longer need this counseling session. We realize now what the problem is in our marriage." She continued, "Our family is under demonic attack, so we decided to love each other more; spend more time together and confront our issues on a unified front rather than attacking each other." I said, "Well, good for you! But you didn't have to drive all the way here to tell me that. You could have simply called and cancelled the appointment." The husband said, "We just made this determination on our way here." He reasoned, "I know this might sound crazy, but while on our way here, we saw a church billboard sign that read, 'Don't let Satan destroy your marriage: Join forces, fight back! The devil is a liar.'" She added, "When we saw that sign we both instantly knew that it articulated our problem and offered the solution. It couldn't have been anyone but God." That was more than 13 years ago and that couple is still happily married.

There is extraordinary power in recognizing the voice of God. In the book of I Samuel, Hannah was depressed because she could not get pregnant. She went to the temple and prayed to God that if He gave her a son she would give him back to God. While she prayed her mouth moved but no words came out. The priest Eli saw her mouth moving but heard no words coming out, and to her face accused her of being drunk. She explained to the priest that she wasn't drunk but was pouring out her heart to God. Eli told her "go, and may God grant you what you have asked for." Hannah recognized the Voice of God through the man of God and believed that it was God speaking to her. Shortly after that she became pregnant and bore Samuel. God gave Hannah a verbal answer to her prayer while she was praying, through the words of Eli. Hannah probably would have missed her blessing if she had not been spiritually alert enough to hear the Voice of God through the man of God (I Samuel 1:9-20).

Today the Faith Challenge requires you to intentionally listen for the Voice of God in every situation in which you find yourself. Listen for God's voice in the music, whether it is sacred or secular. Listen for His voice not only through the Word and private meditation, but also during the regular routine of life. Listen for it on billboards, television programs, books, magazines, newspapers, private conversations, public speeches, or any experience you may have today. You may be asking, "How will I know it is His Voice?" The Lord knew you would ask that question so He answered it in advance, saying, "I have other sheep that are not of this sheep pen. I must bring them also. They too will listen to my voice" (John 10:16 KJV). His sheep know His voice.

---

**The Faith Challenge Day 7**

➤ A 20-minute daily devotion
  1 Scripture reading: I Samuel 1:1-20
  2 Prayer: your prayer should include that God makes you aware of His voice in every encounter today.
  3    A 10-minute meditation: clear your mind and focus on your breathing and listen for the voice of God.
➤ Prayer periods: 9:00am, 12:00pm, 3:00pm and 6:00pm. Spend time in prayer listening for God to speak.

---

## At the End of Day 7

Name three mediums through which you recognized the voice of God.

What was the message you received from the voice of God today?

If you received direction or instruction from the Lord today, how likely are to follow it?

Write your reflections for day 7.

## Sunday Day 8

*"I will worship toward thy holy temple, and praise thy*
*name for thy lovingkindness and for thy truth: for thou hast*
*magnified thy word above all thy name."*
(Psalms 138:2 KJV)

**Today's Challenge:** I will enroll in a Sunday school class at my church. I will attend worship as a true worshipper and not a spectator. I will listen attentively to the sermon and apply it to my life.

Bible study groups, in most instances, are designed to study the Bible for scriptural enlightenment. They serve to expose the students to Bible stories and biblical doctrine. While private study of scripture is necessary, studying in groups has its advantages. You can receive new scriptural insights and fresh biblical commentary from others in the group, which is always helpful. Also, a bond is often formed between the persons in the study group that sometimes leads to deep and profound relationships.

Corporate worship is the high point of the week. It is the time when the entire community comes together and corporately seeks divine intimacy with God in worship. There is a type of revelation that we receive in worship that we don't receive anywhere else. The 6th chapter of the book of Isaiah records that it is in the worship that Isaiah received his call into the prophetic ministry. "In the year that

King Uzziah died, I saw the Lord. He was sitting on his throne, high and exalted, and his robe filled the whole Temple...Then I heard the Lord say, 'Whom shall I send? Who will be our messenger?' I answered, 'I will go! Send me!' So he told me to go and give the people this message..." (Isaiah 6 GNV).

In most cases, it is in the worship services where people hear the gospel message and give their lives to the Lord and are saved. It is in the worship setting where God reveals His will for their lives.

So today, while you worship, listen for God's voice in every aspect of the worship experience.

---

**The Faith Challenge Day 8**

➤ 20-minute daily devotion
1. Scripture reading: Psalm 150
2. Prayer: pray that the Lord prepares you for worship
3. Meditation: 10-minute quiet meditation. Clear your mind and focus on your breathing.

---

## At the End of day 8

Did God speak to you through the music at church today? If not, what do you think prevented it?

Did God speak to you through the sermon? What was God's Word saying to you today? If you didn't receive a Word from God through the sermon, what do you think prevented you from receiving?

What new revelation did you receive today during the worship?

Did you enroll in a Sunday school class? If so, why did you choose that particular class; if not, why?

# Chapter 4

# A Week of Consecration

The second seven days of the Faith Challenge are dedicated to the act of consecration. To consecrate is to set something apart and to declare it holy and sacred. In the Old Testament it was the role of the priest to perform the rites of consecration. But now, through Christ we are all priests and have been empowered to perform the rite of consecration (I Peter 2:9 KJV). Sommer Marsden defines consecration in this way: "To devote solemnly to a purpose." Every relationship, every material possession, every engagement, whether secular or sacred, needs to be consecrated, that is, devoted solemnly to a divine purpose.

All of life's engagements are empowered when the higher purpose for the engagements is discovered. If you were to ask the average couple, "What is the purpose for your relationship or marriage?" Or if you asked the average person, "What is the true purpose for your employment?" Or if you asked the average student,

"What is your true purpose for attending college?" More times than not, the answer would be to accomplish some personal or material goal. The couple might say, "The purpose of our relationship is to make each other happy and to spend the rest of our lives together." The worker might say, "The purpose for my employment is to make a living to provide for myself or my family." The college student might say, "The reason I attend college is to be better equipped for the workforce." All the answers focus on the personal or material and miss the deeper spiritual purpose. If all you want out of a marriage is the temporary, surface reality of happiness, you are truly missing out on all of the riches a marriage has to offer. If the sole purpose for your employment is to make a dollar, you have missed out on the more profound purpose that employment has to offer. If all you want out of your college experience is to acquire a skill set for employment, you have missed a higher purpose of your college experience.

When all my engagements are devoted to a higher, spiritual purpose, I consecrate them to be a spiritual practice. I therefore enter all my engagements as a spiritual practice. Spiritual practice is using every experience as an opportunity for spiritual growth. If spiritual practice is the purpose for your marriage, even in those times when you are not happy in your marriage, if you are growing spiritually your marriage is still accomplishing its higher purpose. If spiritual practice is the purpose for your employment, it becomes far more significant than a mere paycheck, it's glorifying God through your work. If spiritual practice is the purpose of your college experience, the degree becomes less significant than the college experience itself.

In the bestselling book *The Alchemist* by Paulo Coelho, Santiago, a little shepherd boy had dreams of finding treasure near the pyramids of ancient Egypt. He followed his dream. He sold his sheep and left home in search of his dream. His journey was a long one. On his journey he met and made friends with an old king. He met and worked for a merchant for several years. He came in contact with an alchemist. He met and fell madly in love with the beautiful Fatima. Santiago was determined to accomplish his dream. After a long journey he finally arrived at the pyramids and started digging for the treasure. He found the treasure that he had always dreamed of. Immediately after he found the treasure, thus accomplishing his goal, a band of robbers beat him and took the treasure from him. The story ends with Santiago without his long sought-after treasure; with bruised ribs, a swollen face, and a busted and bloody mouth, Santiago looks up at the pyramids, laughing with praise, because he finally discovered that the journey to find the treasure was much more valuable than the treasure itself! Santiago realized at the end of his journey that his entire journey was a spiritual practice.

For the next seven days, the Faith Challenge requires that we consecrate all our encounters and relationships to God as a spiritual practice.

# Monday Day 9

*"Keep on loving one another as brothers and sisters. Don't*
*forget to show hospitality to strangers..."*
(Hebrews 13:1-2)NIV

**Today's Challenge:** I consecrate all of my personal relationships to God as a spiritual practice.

When you intentionally appreciate all your personal relationships as a spiritual practice, it immediately adds a new depth to your relationships. All your partners, whether they are your children, spouse, lover, friend, relatives, become your teachers who teach you about yourself and your relationship with God. Gary Zukav has suggested that, "Spiritual partnership is partnership between equals for the purpose of spiritual growth."[20]

My son and daughter, young adults now, have been two of my greatest teachers. I used to find it difficult to exercise patience. One of my daily prayers was for God to teach me patience. God sent my children into my life for many reasons, one of which was to teach me the patience that I prayed for. Their upbringing was far more privileged than mine. In fact, I was raised in poverty. Being raised in that impoverished environment dramatically accelerated my maturation. I had to learn early in life to do things for myself and

---

[20] Gary Zukav, *Spiritual Partnership*. Pg. 135.

never to expect anyone to do anything for me. Looking back over my life, I feel like I have been an adult since I was 14 years old. My children, however, were raised in a relatively affluent community with both parents deeply involved in their lives. Their mother is an educator with a master's degree and their father, a pastor of a mega church with a doctoral degree. Their environment was far different from mine. I would often become frustrated with them because of their apparent immaturity. Being the educator, my wife would constantly remind me that I was mature beyond my years because of my upbringing, and that I could not expect our children to be as responsible as I was at 12 or 13 years of age. She cautioned me that their attitudes and level of maturity was age-appropriate and that I needed to be more patient with them. My children became my teacher who taught me how to exercise patience. Because of them I have become more patient, not only with them but in every area of my life.

People who are close to you can reveal the areas in your life wherein you need further development. If jealousy is a problem area in your life, and you have been trying to rid yourself of it, you won't know how you are progressing in that area until you are challenged in that area. Jealousy is more intense among people who are closest to you. When someone close to you has good success or sudden fortune, if you feel jealous, that person has just taught you that you don't have the jealousy issue under control like you may have thought, and more work is needed in that area.

When we appreciate our relationships as a spiritual practice, we never blame others for making us feel a certain way. That is, we no longer say to the other person things like "You made me mad!" Or, "You hurt my feelings." When relationships become a spiritual practice, the questions are no longer posed outward but the questions are now directed inward. No one has so much power in your life to make you feel a certain way if you choose not to feel that way. If you are "mad" or have "hurt feelings" it is because you chose those emotions as your response to what the other person did or said. So the new question becomes, "Why did I choose to be mad?" Or, "why did I choose to have hurt feelings?" These questions will cause you to investigate yourself.

Our congregation completed construction of a new church facility. The congregation is very proud of the accomplishment and pleased with the new facility. After being in the new building less than a year, there was a heavy rain, and part of the building flooded. Most of the leadership of the church didn't get angry at the rain for flooding the building, but we investigated to understand why the building responded to the rain by flooding. Because of the rain, we found that there was a flaw in the design that needed to be corrected. Relationships as a spiritual practice are designed to reveal to you where you are flawed so that you may begin to correct it.

Today you will appreciate your relationships as a spiritual practice.

---

**The Faith Challenge Day 9**

➤ 20-minute daily devotion
    1 Scripture reading: John 13:31-35
    2 Prayer: pray that God will give you insight as to how to appreciate all your relationships as spiritual practices.
    3 Meditation: 10-minute quiet meditation. Clear your mind and focus on your breathing and listen for the voice of God to provide direction for your life.
➤ Food fast from 8:00am to 8:00pm
➤ Today also abstain from the internet, television, radio, and any other form of electronic entertainment, unless of course it is required for your job.
➤ Also with fasting today you must pray at least four times: at 9:00am, 12:00pm, 3:00pm and 6:00pm. Your prayer should include asking God to bless your relationships.

# At the End of Day 9

What are three ways you think your personal relationships will change if you appreciate them as spiritual practices.

## Tuesday Day 10

*"Be not forgetful to entertain strangers: for thereby some have entertained angels unawares."* (Hebrews 13:2KJV)

**Today's Challenge:** I will consecrate all of my casual unanticipated encounters with others as a divinely-arranged spiritual practice.

As I sat at the airport waiting to board the plane, I was totally distracted and intensely annoyed by the most unruly, insubordinate, out-of-control child I have ever seen. This child's behavior was so bad that the authorities from the airline warned the mother that if she could not get her child under control, they would not be allowed to board the plane. By boarding time the mother was not able to get the child to calm down. The boarding passengers were all relieved, because we assumed that since the mother could not get the child under control they would not be allowed to board. We were finally getting away from this irate child. I boarded the plane and sat comfortably in first class, ordered a cup of coffee, and turned on my iPad to finish reading an interesting book. I looked up, and to my dismay, right next to me were seated the mother and her outrageous child! I immediately started praying and asking God what had I done to deserve this punishment? Of all the seats on this plane, why did God divinely arrange for me to be seated next to the most contemptible little boy known to man, for a two-hour flight? During the flight this kid's ranting and antics got so outrageous that the passengers were totally disturbed and complained to the flight attendants. It got so out of hand that the co-pilot personally came to the mother and warned that if she couldn't get a handle on it he would be forced to land the plane and put them off. But I was the lucky one, I got to sit right next to him for two hours. The flight was full so I couldn't change seats. Everyone on the plane pitied me. The airline even gave me a free round trip ticket to anywhere in the continental United States for enduring this torture. Through all of this, the man in the seat in front of us seemed to be undisturbed by the drama created by the boy. He was reading the paper and drinking apple juice with such calm and serenity. I asked him how was he able to maintain his composure through all of this? He said, "I have learned that nothing can disturb or distract me unless I let it." He continued, "If you would focus on the book you are reading and take your attention off the kid, you'll soon forget he's even on the plane." He concluded, "Your being disturbed is not about the kid, it's about you." With that he went back to reading his paper and drinking his apple juice, unbothered. I decided to take his advice. I focused on the book I was reading and took my focus off the child and soon I got so enthralled by the book that the child faded far into the background of my experience. For the next hour and fifteen minutes, I enjoyed the flight undisturbed by the child.

The out-of-control child and the calm man on the plane were both strangers to me. For two hours they were both sent into my life to teach me a valuable skill that I practice almost every day of my life: that trivial matters will arise in life and the more attention we give to the trivial, the bigger and more disturbing they will become. But if you intentionally change your focus to what you deem important, the triviality will fade into the background. The only things that can disturb you are the things you choose to allow to disturb you.

Casual encounters are often rich with important spiritual insights that we will miss, unless we appreciate them as a spiritual practice. Today, in every casual encounter you have, look for the spiritual insight. You may not understand the meaning of the encounter right away, but at some point, if you are spiritually sensitive enough, it will be revealed.

---

**The Faith Challenge Day 10**

➤ A 20-minute daily devotion
  1. Scripture reading: Hebrews 13:1-7
  2. Prayer: your prayer should include that God reveals the meaning of each encounter with others.
  3. A 10-minute meditation: clear your mind and focus on your breathing, and listen for the voice of God.
➤ Prayer periods: 9:00am, 12:00pm, 3:00pm and 6:00pm. Spend time in prayer listening for God to speak.
➤ If tonight is your church's mid-week worship night, you are to attend.

---

# At the End of Day 10

Identify three unexpected encounters you had today and describe what they revealed to you about yourself or about God.

# Wednesday Day 11

*"...Whatever you do, do it all for the glory of God."*
(I Corinthians 10:31NIV)

**Today's Challenge:** I will approach my job, school, housework, job search, daily chores, and any other tasks as a spiritual practice.

Jesus said, "Blessed are the pure in heart for they shall see God" (Matthew 5:8KJV). God is constantly present and at work in every situation. However, only the pure in heart can recognize His presence and understand that God is at work. Brother Lawrence of France recognized God's presence in every engagement. In fact, he referred to it as "Practicing the Presence of God." Brother Lawrence was born in Herimenil, France, in 1614. He sincerely desired to enter the priesthood but he was refused because he did not have adequate academic training. He therefore entered the priory in Paris as a lay brother. He spent a great deal of his life serving in the priory as a lowly kitchen worker. Despite his lowly position at the priory, he developed a reputation for experiencing profound peace. Visitors from near and far came to get counsel from this lowly kitchen worker. He attributed his deep peace and unspeakable joy to his ability to practice the presence of God in all of life's situations.[21]

---

[21] Wikipedia, http://en.wikipedia.org/wiki/Brother_Lawrence.

When we become aware that God is always present with us, even during our employment, and seeks to get the glory out of it, it empowers our work. For many people, after their morning devotional period they go about their work and think no more about God until their next devotional period. But to be mindful of God's loving presence in the midst of our daily engagements adds special significance to our work. It adds more profound purpose to work. Practicing God's presence in our daily work will cause us to take pride in the quality of our work. Practicing the presence of God will take the stress and tension out of the daily grind because you are no longer working simply for a paycheck or for the sake of just "getting the task done," you are now doing it to the glory of God and therein lies peace. It is said of Brother Lawrence that, "Even when he was busiest in the kitchen, it was evident that the brother's spirit was dwelling in God. He often did the work that two usually did, but he never seemed to bustle. Rather, he gave each chore the time that it required, always preserving his modest and tranquil air, working neither slowly nor swiftly, dwelling in calmness of soul and unalterable peace."[22]

I talk to people regularly who hate their daily engagements. They hate their jobs, school, homework, housework, daily chores, etc. And because they hate their daily engagements so much, they tend to resist them. Resisting what is only creates deeper frustration. If they would but change their attitudes towards their daily engage-

---

[22] Brother Lawrence, *The Brother Lawrence Collection*. Pg. 1538.

ments from a dreadful task to a spiritual practice, recognize God's presence and help in their employment, engage God in conversation while they work, and remember that God seeks glory out of it, it can transform their entire experience. Brother Lawrence says, "Our transformation did not depend upon changing our work, but in doing that for God's sake, which we commonly do for our own."[23]

Approach all your daily engagements with same reverence and awe with which you approach your daily devotion and begin to enjoy God at a level you never knew was available.

---

**The Faith Challenge Day 11**

➤ A 20-minute daily devotion
1. Scripture reading: Galatians 5:16-25
2. Prayer: your prayer should include thanking God for selecting you to perform your particular task to His glory.
3. A 10-minute meditation: clear your mind and focus on your breathing, and listen for the voice of God.

➤ Prayer periods: 9:00am, 12:00pm, 3:00pm and 6:00pm. Spend time in prayer listening for God to speak.

➤ If tonight is your church's mid-week worship night, you are to attend.

---

[23] Brother Lawrence, *The Practice of the Presence of God*. Pg. 160.

# At the End of Day 11

Discuss three ways that approaching your tasks as a spiritual practice today influence how you performed them.

# Thursday Day 12

*"Seek the LORD and his strength, seek his face continu-
ally."* (I Chronicles 16:11KJV)

**Today's Challenge:** I will appreciate all of my reading materials,
television and radio programs, internet, and all other media expo-
sures as a spiritual practice.

To seek God's face continually, as David says in I Chronicles
16:11, is to anticipate divine revelation in all things. Jeffery Johnson,
pastor of the Eastern Star Church in Indianapolis, Indiana has an
extensive collection of news articles that he has cut out of various
newspapers and magazines over the years. From these articles he
extracts illustrations for preaching and teaching. He allows God to
reveal lessons that enhance his understanding of reality, and he passes
those valuable lessons on to his congregants through preaching and
teaching.

The movie *Good Will Hunting,* starring Matt Damon and Robin
Williams, is one of my favorites. I am deeply moved by this movie
not only because of the brilliant acting and powerful plot, but also
because it gave me greater insight and more compassion for those
who have been orphaned and abused in their childhoods. It pro-
foundly informed how I approach ministry to foster families who
have taken in abused children. I allowed God to speak to me through

that particular medium and it added an important insight I don't think I would have acquired otherwise.

My sister-in-law and I were engaged in a deep conversation about romantic relationships as we drove in my car. As my car radio played softly in the background, she explained her frustration about not being able to find a suitable mate. She is a beautiful Christian woman who loves the Lord, is gainfully employed, a homeowner, and she successfully raised three beautiful daughters who are now grown and are making lives for themselves. As we engaged in conversation about her loneliness, a song came on the radio. We both sat in silence while we listened to lyrics of the song. The song is entitled, "Wait for Love" by Luther Vandross. The chorus of the song says, "Wait for love, that you've been missing; sometimes loves takes a long time; but wait for love and you're gonna get your chance to love; wait for love, wait for love." After the song ended, she asked me if I thought it was a coincidence that this song came on right in the middle of our conversation. I told her that I don't believe in coincidences. She then asked, did I think the lyrics of that song could be God's way of answering her question? I told her that God can do anything and can speak through any medium He chooses, for God is all powerful! I told her that the important thing is not whether I believed that is God speaking to her, but does she believe it? She embraced that moment as God speaking to her about her frustration. She decided to go about her daily life and stop complaining about her loneliness and simply "wait for love," as the song suggested. Exactly one year later she fell in love with a wonderful gentleman and they are now planning their wedding. She opened up and allowed God to speak peace and make a promise to her through a love song. She enjoyed the peace and has received the promise. If the Lord can speak through Balaam's jackass, surely He can speak through a love song (Numbers 22:28).

---

**The Faith Challenge Day 12**

➤ A 20-minute daily devotion
  1 Scripture reading: Numbers 22:21-35
  2 Prayer: your prayer should include that God gives you revelation through your exposure to all types of media.
  3 A 10-minute meditation: clear your mind and focus on your breathing and listen for the voice of God.
➤ Prayer periods: 9:00am, 12:00pm, 3:00pm and 6:00pm. Spend time in prayer listening for God to speak.
➤ If tonight is your church's mid-week worship night, you are to attend.

---

# At the End of Day 12

What did your exposure to the media reveal to you about yourself and your relationship with God?

# Friday Day 13

*"Jesus took the bread and blessed it."* (Matthew 26:26NIV)

**Today's Challenge:** I will bless all things that made it possible for me to have food and drink, thus making eating a spiritual practice.

We can become so absorbed in our daily activities that we sometimes forget how blessed we actually are to have food and clean water. Today the Faith Challenge calls your attention to the following sobering facts concerning the problem of hunger. Hopefully, after consideration of these facts you will begin to appreciate your daily bread as a spiritual practice.

- Every year 15 million children die of hunger.
- Throughout the 1990s, more than 100 million children died from illness and starvation. One in twelve people worldwide is malnourished, including 160 million children under the age of 5.
- The Indian subcontinent has nearly half the world's hungry people. Africa and the rest of Asia together have approximately 40%, and the remaining hungry people are found in Latin America and other parts of the world.
- Nearly one in four people, 1.3 billion, live on less than $1 per day.

- 3 billion people in the world today struggle to survive on US$2/day.
- In 1994, the Urban Institute in Washington DC estimated that one out of 6 elderly people in the U.S. has an inadequate diet.
- In the U.S., hunger and race are related. In 1991, 46% of African-American children were chronically hungry, and 40% of Latino children were chronically hungry.
- The infant mortality rate is closely linked to inadequate nutrition among pregnant women. The U.S. ranks 23rd among industrial nations in infant mortality. African-American infants die at nearly twice the rate of white infants.
- One out of every eight children under the age of twelve in the U.S. goes to bed hungry every night.
- Half of all children under five years of age in South Asia, and one-third of those in sub-Saharan Africa, are malnourished.
- Malnutrition is implicated in more than half of all child deaths worldwide - a proportion unmatched by any infectious disease since the Black Death.
- About 183 million children weigh less than they should for their age.
- Every 3.6 seconds, someone dies of hunger.
- It is estimated that some 800 million people in the world suffer from hunger.[24]

---

[24] An End to World Hunger and Hope for the Future: http://library.thinkquest.org/C002291/intro.htm

When you sit down to have a meal today, keep those who are dying of starvation in mind, and whisper a prayer for them. Before you begin to eat, bless God for providing you with food and drink. Bless those who prepared your meal and brought it to your table. Pierre Pradervand has suggested that we should even go so far as to "Bless the cashier at the checkout counter of the supermarket. The drivers and transporters who brought the food to the store... the Mexican laborers who harvested your California tomatoes, the Kenyan and Indonesian peasant farmers who produced the coffee... the farmer from Indiana who grew the wheat for the bread. The chance is that long before you have finished your meal, you will have cast a web of blessings that cover the planet and even beyond."[25]

---

**The Faith Challenge Day 13**

➢ A 20-minute daily devotion
   1. Scripture reading: John 21:1-14
   2. Prayer: your prayer should include sending blessings to everyone and everything that make it possible for you to have food. You should also pray for those who are suffering from hunger.
   3. A 10-minute meditation: clear your mind and focus on your breathing and listen for the voice of God.
➢ Prayer periods: 9:00am, 12:00pm, 3:00pm and 6:00pm. Your prayers should send blessing to the hungry and gratitude for your food.

---

[25] Pradervand, Pg. 66.

# At the End of Day 13

How did reflecting on all the hunger in the world impact how you appreciated the food you enjoyed today?

How did reflecting on how your food got from the point of origin all the way to you influence your appreciation for your food today?

## Saturday Day 14

*"'How do you know about me?' Nathanael asked. And*
*Jesus replied, 'I could see you under the fig tree.'"*
(John 1:48NLT)

**Today's Challenge:** Today I will make a spiritual practice of my leisure.

Jesus noticed Nathanael under the fig tree and described him as "An honest man..." What was Nathanael doing under the fig tree that would cause Jesus to portray him as an honest man? The text is unclear as to his activity under the fig tree, however it was a common practice in their culture to relax in the shade of the heavy foliage of the fig tree while eating figs. It is likely that Jesus noticed Nathanael in his leisure and deemed him an honest man. Nathanael's leisure time, like all leisure, forced him into the present moment and it is only in the present that we experience the presence of God.

Leisure can be an extremely powerful time in our lives. Whether we spend our leisure playing a round of golf or a game of tennis, or swimming, mountain climbing, horseback riding, jogging, exercising, sitting on the beach, taking a casual stroll, or just simply relaxing, the one thing they all have in common is that they demand our full attention which forces us into the present moment.

I have several colleagues who are avid golfers. They describe golf as the most relaxing activity they participate in. Since I am not a golfer I could not understand how swinging a stick at a little white ball with the goal of knocking it into a small hole in the ground could be relaxing. I have a very close friend who has taken an intense interest in mountain climbing. When I asked him what the fascination is about mountain climbing, he said for some reason it relaxes him. My passion is shooting pool and I find that it relaxes me so much I can literally play pool for hours and not even notice the passing of time. Playing golf, shooting pool, rock or mountain climbing, and other leisure activities demand that all your attention is intensely focused on the present moment. It is not the round of golf, or the pool shooting, or the mountain climbing that's causing the relaxation, but it is simply being in the present moment. You cannot be preoccupied with the past or be projected into the future and focus on hitting that golf ball, or climbing the mountain, or hitting a cue ball at the same time. In these precious moments the present is not reduced to a means to an end, but the present moment becomes the end in itself.

Make a spiritual practice of your leisure by going deeply into the activity you are engaged in. By going deeply into it you move more deeply into the present moment. It is only in the present moment can we fully experience the love and power of God.

**The Faith Challenge Day 14**
➢ A 20-minute daily devotion
  1. Scripture reading: John 1:43-51
  2. Prayer: your prayer should include that God makes you spiritually sensitive enough to hear His voice during your leisure.
  3. A 10-minute meditation: clear your mind and focus on your breathing and listen for the voice of God.
➢ Prayer periods: 9:00am, 12:00pm, 3:00pm and 6:00pm. Spend time in prayer listening for God to speak.

# At the End of Day 14

Describe your leisure time today and how it better helped you understand yourself and your relationship with God.

# Sunday Day 15

*"They that worship Him must worship Him in Spirit and in truth for they are the kind of worshippers that the Father seeks."* (John 4:23NIV)

**Today's Challenge:** Today I will make my worship a spiritual practice.

The woman at the well in John Chapter 4 seemed to be more interested in the place of worship than the power of worship. She told Jesus, "Our fathers worshipped in this mountain, 'Mt. Gerizm,' but you say Jerusalem is the place where men ought to worship." For far too many people, the place of worship becomes far more important than the power that true worship has to offer. With the continually growing list of mega churches, and the shrinking list of small community-based churches, people are more and more identifying with popular churches simply because of their high-profile. Many of these members tend to boast more about their popular church and their glamorous pastor than they do about the deeper reality of encountering God within the holy context of community worship. These deeper issues are rarely taken into consideration when people join these mega churches. Many of the people who join do so because it is the "in thing" to do. I am not berating our mega churches because they do meet a tremendous need in the community. I know firsthand, because the church that I pastor is considered a mega church. For many of our congregants, Sunday morning worship is a time for socializing, networking, and true worship takes a backseat to the trivial and minutia which rob the worship experience of the power and the revelation that God intended for worship.

Today, whether the church you attend is a mega church or a small church, the important element to focus on is actually encountering God and receiving revelation that only God can give in the worship experience.

In the second chapter of the Gospel of Luke there is a story of a man named Simeon. The Bible describes him as "just and devoted, waiting for the consolation of Israel." This man was in the temple worshipping. While he worshipped he was looking for the Lord's arrival. On this particular worship day, Mary and Joseph brought Jesus to the temple to be circumcised. Simeon finally got what he had been waiting for, his chance to embrace Christ.

When we go to worship with positive anticipation, we will always find special revelation that we would have not found had we not gone to worship expecting something positive.

---

**The Faith Challenge Day 15**
- ➢ 20-minute daily devotion
    1. Scripture reading: John 4:1-24
    2. Prayer: pray that the Lord gives you the ability to worship Him in Spirit and in Truth.
    3. 10 minute meditation. Focus on you breathing and listen for the voice of God.

---

# At the End of Day 15

What special revelation did you receive today in worship? If you did not receive any special revelation in worship today, why do you think you did not?

# Chapter 5

# A Week of Compassion

M atthew Fox once wrote, "Compassion is not sentiment but is making justice and doing works of mercy. Compassion is not a moral commandment but a flow and overflow of the fullest human and divine energies." Compassion is love in action. Jesus sums up compassion best by saying, "Do unto others as you would have them do unto you." This statement made by the Master is known as the Golden Rule.

The Golden Rule suggests that you don't wait for someone to treat you a certain way before you treat that person the way you want to be treated. That is, the person exercising the Golden Rule becomes the initiator. So all the people you come in contact with are treated the way you would want to be treated. It sounds simple, but it is difficult for many people to practice because most people think they are a little better than most of the people they come in contact with. Most people think they are a little smarter, holier, more spiritual, better looking, better educated, more sophisticated than the average person they come in contact with. That being the case, we often feel justified in our maltreatment of others because we feel we have a right, since we are better than they are. The Golden Rule sounds extremely simple but it is literally impossible to practice if you are a carnal-dominated person.

This is a radical notion, because it suggests that we are not to allow others to define how we treat them based upon how they treat us, but it is based upon how we want to be treated. Jesus said this one principle sums up the entire Old Testament.

What criterion do you use to determine how you treat others? Do you let their status in the community determine it for you? Do you let their financial position determine it? Do you base it on their looks, pedigree or educational attainment? The truth is, we treat people differently on the basis of a variety of variables. But the Golden Rule demands that the only criterion in how you treat people is how you want to be treated; that is love in action, this is the essence of compassion.

# Monday Day 16

*"May the Lord show kindness to you as you have shown kindness to me…"* (Ruth 1:8NIV)

**Today's challenge:** Spend one hour in a nursing home praying for and reading scriptures to the residents.

The elderly in the American culture are not as valued and honored as they should be, or as they are in other cultures. They are certainly not as revered as they were in biblical culture. The elderly were highly esteemed in biblical culture. They were valued for their wisdom, looked to for advice, and provided leadership for the community.

The story of Naomi and Ruth is a perfect picture of how we are to look after our senior citizens. Naomi had a tough life in Moab. She lost her husband and both of her sons to death. She decided to leave Moab and return to Bethlehem, her home town. Her daughter-in-law Ruth refused to leave her and promised to take care of her, "Don't ask me to leave you! Let me go with you. Wherever you go, I will go; wherever you live, I will live. Your people will be my people, and your God will be my God. Wherever you die, I will die, and that is where I will be buried. May the Lord's worst punishment come upon me if I let anything but death separate me from you" (Ruth 1:16-17GNV).

Today you will show your love to a senior citizen in a nursing

home, and perhaps even adopt your own Naomi.

---

**The Faith Challenge Day 16**
- ➤ 20-minute daily devotion
    1. Scripture reading: James 1:21-27
    2. Prayer: a segment of your prayer should be for the nursing home residents you are going to visit today.
    3. Meditation: 10-minute quiet meditation. Clear your mind and focus on your breathing and listen for the voice of God to provide direction for your life.
- ➤ Food fast from 8:00am to 8:00pm.
- ➤ Today also abstain from the internet, television, radio, and any other form of electronic entertainment, unless of course it is required for your job.
- ➤ Prayer periods: 9:00am, 12:00pm, 3:00pm and 6:00pm. Your prayers should be for the residents.

# At the End of Day 16

Describe your experience and your feelings while you ministered at the nursing home today.

Were you aware of God's presence while you were there? Explain.

## Tuesday Day 17

*"I was sick and you looked after me…*
*Whatever you did to the least one of these brothers of mine*
*you did it for me."* (Matthew 25:36 &40NIV)

**Today's Challenge**: Find a member of your church or someone that you do not have a very close relationship with who is in the hospital and visit.

In December of 2006, I spent 13 days in the hospital after undergoing open heart surgery. One of the greatest sources of inspiration for me was to see all the people coming to visit me. People I didn't know came to see me and read the scriptures, and sang songs to me and prayed for me. Just to know that someone cared enough to take time out of their schedule and drive to the hospital, just to visit me, gave me a boost of energy that I believe contributed to my total recovery.

As a pastor, my pastoral responsibilities include hospital visitations. While visiting the person I specifically came to see, I often stop and visit with people who are in their rooms all alone. I tell them that I am a pastor and ask if they mind if I come in and read scripture and pray for them, and perhaps even sit and chat with them for a short while. These unexpected visits always bring a smile to the patient and lift my own spirit.

**The Faith Challenge Day 17**

➤ A 20-minute daily devotion
   1. Scripture reading: Matthew 25:31-46
   2. Prayer: your prayer should be for the people you are scheduled to visit today.
   3. A 10-minute meditation: clear your mind and focus on your breathing and listen for the voice of God.
➤ Prayer periods: 9:00am, 12:00pm, 3:00pm and 6:00pm. Your prayers should be for the sick.
➤ If tonight is your church's mid-week worship night, you are to attend.

# At the End of Day 17

Who did you visit in the hospital today?

How long did you stay?

What did this visit reveal to you about yourself and your relationship with God?

# Wednesday Day 18

*"For I was hungry and you gave me something to eat."*
(Matthew 25:35NIV)

**Today's Challenge:** Take food to the local food pantry or go grocery shopping for a family in need.

The late Dr. S. Leon Whitney, former pastor of the Prospect Baptist Church in Detroit, Michigan, would often tell a fascinating story about how God provided for his family when he was a child. His mother worked a full-time job and was a part-time student in college and full-time single mother of five children. He recounts one week his mother had several unexpected emergency expenses which caused her to run out of money before she could buy food for the family. She believed that God would provide for the family, but didn't see how He would do it. Dinner time came and passed without food. She and her children retired to bed that evening without eating. Dr. Whitney recalls not being able to fall asleep because of the noise of his growling stomach, coupled with the noise of squeaking floorboards from his mother pacing the floor in her bedroom. All at once, the squeaking floorboards stopped and dead silence fell over the house. Disturbed by the silence, he got up to check on his mother. He peeped into her bedroom and witnessed her on her knees in prayer. He returned to bed and fell fast asleep, only to be aroused at

11:00pm out of his sleep by the smell of bacon, eggs, biscuits, and the voice of his mother singing. He went to the kitchen and found his mother preparing a meal for the family. When he asked how it happened, she told him that her brother had gone grocery shopping for the family. She further explained that she didn't call her brother and ask for anything, but that her brother said he felt compelled by the Lord to bless his sister and nieces and nephews with a week's worth of groceries. She told him to wake the other children and tell them dinner was ready. God often uses those who are obedient to Him to be His vessel of blessing to others.

Today the Faith Challenge requires that you avail yourself to be a blessing to someone in need.

---

### The Faith Challenge Day 18

- ➢ A 20-minute daily devotion
  1. Scripture reading: Matthew 25:31-46
  2. Prayer: your prayer should be for the hungry, the food pantry you are going to bless today with food, or for the family for whom you have prayerfully chosen to shop.
  3. A 10-minute meditation: clear your mind and focus on your breathing and listen for the voice of God.
- ➢ Prayer periods: 9:00am, 12:00pm, 3:00pm and 6:00pm. A segment of your prayers should be intercessory for the food pantry or the family you chose to bless.
- ➢ If tonight is your church's mid-week worship night, you are to attend.

---

# At the End of Day 18

Did you take food to a shelter or did you grocery shop for a family?

Did you experience joy in giving today? If yes describe the experience in detail. If not, why do you think there was no joy in your giving?

How do you believe God feels about your giving today?

# Thursday Day 19

*"I was in prison and you visited me."* (Matthew 25:36NIV)

**Today's Challenge:** Visit someone who is incarcerated.

This challenge is not to be confused with starting a prison ministry. A prison ministry has a specific mission. Most prison ministries' missions are to conduct regular worship services, substitute for the chaplain when he is not available, conduct Bible studies, distribute literature and Bibles, help those with addictions, prepare those coming out of prison with community reentry, etc. Prison ministries are extremely important and have blessed many inmates and their families and communities. However, today's challenge has nothing to do with prison ministry but it has to do with blessing an inmate with your presence, love, and authentic concern. You are not asked to conduct a Bible study, or give the inmate any advice as to how he can better his life, or preach to and teach the inmate. This challenge does not require you to stand in judgment of the inmate but to relate to the inmate as a human being, your equal.

The carnal nature will vehemently resist this challenge. The carnal nature cannot fathom the notion that you are equal to a prison inmate. The carnal nature needs people around whose life situations are worse than its own. The carnal nature cannot separate a person's life from his life situation. A person's life and life situation are totally different. A person's life is the actual spirit with which God has empowered every human being. Therefore, all human beings are equal. The quality of spirit or life does not vary in degrees of greatness from one person to the next. The life or spirit of the three year old Somalian child whose stomach is swollen from malnutrition and is on the brink of death is no greater or lesser than the President of the United States or the Prince of Wales. What is different, however, is their life situations. The carnal nature values people according to their life situations, rather than the life or spirit that God has given equally to all. Jesus said, "A man's life does not consist in the abundance of his possessions" (Luke 12:15NIV). The word used for life here is the Greek term *zoe,* which is the divinely given energy that empowers or animates every living soul and is equal among all people.

Prison inmates may be guilty of crimes and are justly paying their debts to society, but that only represents their life situations. The fact that they are alive suggests that they still have spirit or life or *zoe.* You do not have more life or spirit than they do; your life situation may be better than theirs, but your life is equal to theirs.

This challenge requires you to be there with the inmate, to recognize your equality with the inmate and relate according to the spirit rather than the life situation. Remember, Jesus intimates that He and that inmate are so closely identified, that what you do for the inmate you have done it unto the Lord.

When you visit, talk to the inmate about his life, his feelings, and his family. Discuss his concerns, his dreams, and his aspirations. Your job is to be fully present and to emanate so much love that the inmate actually feels it.

---

**The Faith Challenge Day 19**

➢ A 20-minute daily devotion
  1. Scripture reading: Matthew 25:31-46
  2. Prayer: your prayer should be for the inmate that you are going to visit today.
  3. 10-minute meditation: clear your mind and focus on your breathing and listen for the voice of God.
➢ Prayer periods: 9:00am, 12:00p, 3:00pm and 6:00pm. Pray for those who are incarcerated.
➢ If tonight is your church's mid-week worship night, you are to attend.

---

## At the End of Day 19

Who did you visit incarcerated today?

Do you feel you made a connection with person you visited? If yes, explain in detail. If not, why?

# Friday Day 20

*"Bless those who curse you."* (Luke 6:28NIV)

**Today's Challenge:** Buy a pleasant greeting card and give it to a person you think dislikes you, or the person who irritates you the most.

Jesus said, "Love your enemies," which is to say have no enemies. We have the power to choose whether or not to have enemies, and if we decide to have enemies we are given the freedom to choose who our enemies are. I have decided to use my power to not choose anyone to be my enemy. I therefore have no enemies. Now this doesn't mean that there are others who have not chosen me to be their enemy.

People tend to waste valuable energy on their enemies. Rhonda Byrnes, author of the bestselling book *The Secret,* cites a research experiment in which competitive sprinters were hooked up to biofeedback monitoring equipment and were told to imagine running in a race. The researchers found that the same muscles fired in the same sequence as if the sprinters were actually running. There was a bodily response to an imaginary situation. The body literally exerted energy in response to a thought. When you spend time having imaginary encounters and mental arguments with an enemy, you are expending good energy and the body has only so much energy to expend. Why use up important energy on someone you chose to be an enemy, when that energy can be channeled toward positive things like enhancing your health, or building your career, or improving your marriage, or raising your children? Furthermore, your fueling hatred towards an enemy only exacerbates an already negative situation, in which case no one wins but the devil.

The Faith Challenge calls on you to take appropriate steps to diffuse the negativity that may exists between you and someone else. If you are resistant to this idea and refuse to exercise this challenge, that could be a sign that you are still under the control of your carnal nature. It is only if you have submitted yourself to the authority of the spirit that you will be able to carry out this challenge.

---

**The Faith Challenge Day 20**
➢ A 20-minute daily devotion
   1. Scripture reading: Luke 6:23-33
   2. Prayer: in your prayer send your love and blessings to the person who irritates you the most.
   3. A 10-minute meditation: clear your mind and focus on your breathing and listen for the voice of God.
➢ Prayer periods: 9:00am, 12:00pm, 3:00pm and 6:00pm. Your prayers should be for the person/people who made you an enemy.

---

# At the End of Day 20

Who did you buy a card for today?

Describe the details of your giving the person the card, and how the person responded.

How did the experience make you feel?

# Saturday Day 21

*"I was a stranger and you took me in."*
(Matthew 25:35NIV)

**Today's Challenge:** Visit a homeless shelter and befriend a resident.

The older we become, the less likely we are to enter into new platonic relationships. Some researchers have found that unless the there is a drastic change in our life situation, like relocating to a new city or changing jobs or joining a new church, by the time the average person reaches 40 years of age, his close circles of friends is likely to remain the same. We are far less prone to enter into deep and profound platonic relationships after the age of 40.

Should you defy the odds and enter into a profound platonic relationship after the age of 40, it is highly likely that it will be with someone with whom you have strong particular commonalities, or because the person has something you want.

Today, the Faith Challenge requires that you visit a homeless shelter and visit with someone you've never met before and enter into a friendship with that person. Relate to the homeless person as a human being. Our carnal inclination is to have a superiority complex to the homeless person. Operating under the carnal, you will feel a need to tell this person how to get his life in order, and how to have a relationship with God, and other things that he "needs" to do.

You will be tempted to be condescending simply because the person lives in a shelter and you don't. The homeless person will immediately sense your condescension and will be turned off, and will resist your gestures to establish a friendship. But if you approach this person with respect and genuine love, viewing him as an equal, he or she will be more likely to welcome your offer of friendship.

This challenge is also impossible to accomplish if you are operating under the influence of the carnal nature. The carnal nature will never allow you to make friends with someone "beneath you." Only in the Spirit will you be able to relate to such a person as simply a human being who is not unlike yourself.

---

**The Faith Challenge Day 21**

➢ A 20-minute daily devotion
  1. Scripture reading: Matthew 25:31-46
  2. Prayer: your prayer should be that God will lead you to the resident in the shelter who needs you the most.
  3. A 10-minute meditation: clear your mind and focus on your breathing and listen for the voice of God.
➢ Prayer periods: 9:00am, 12:00pm, 3:00pm and 6:00pm. Pray for the homeless shelter residents.

---

# At the End of Day 21

Describe the person you visited with today at the homeless shelter.

Do you think you made a spiritual connection with the person? If yes, explain. If not, why?

## Sunday Day 22

*"But encourage one another daily, as long as it
is called Today."* (Hebrews 3:13NIV)

**Today's Challenge:** Today at church, speak in a positive and complimentary way to everyone you encounter.

During my college days I served as youth minister at a church in Richmond, Virginia for two years. The Sunday I was to be introduced to the church as the new youth minister, I drove into the church parking lot. As I entered the church, there was an elderly lady walking on a cane, entering the building at the same time. As I held the door open for her I complimented her stylish hat and told her how beautiful she looked in it. She smiled and thanked me for the compliment.

After two years I resigned as youth minister to take a full pastorate at a small rural church. My last day as youth minister, as I said farewell to the membership, the same elderly woman I had complimented two years earlier pulled me to the side and made a confession that has left a lasting impression on me. She said, "The day you were introduced as youth minister of the church was my first Sunday visiting this church. I had been diagnosed with breast cancer and was looking for a faith community to help me shore up my faith to face my challenge. I had visited three different churches in as many weeks, and that particular Sunday was my first time visiting this church. When you held the door open for me and paid me that wonderful compliment, I was almost convinced that this was the church for me. When you were introduced as youth minister, that sealed the deal for me. I knew this was the church for me. Since then I brought my two daughters and my grandchildren, and we have been active members ever since. And if your new church weren't so far away, I would definitely follow you and become a member."

The pastor and other leaders in the church are not the only ones who are called to be sources of inspiration to others. We are all called to encourage and inspire others. Paul makes it clear to the church at Thessalonica, "Therefore encourage one another and build each other up" (I Thessalonians 5:11NIV).

---

**The Faith Challenge Day 22**

➢ 20-minute daily devotion
  1. Scripture reading: 1Peter 3:8-18
  2. Prayer: pray that the Lord might lead you to the people who need encouragement with a word they need to lift them.
  3. Meditation: 10-minute quiet meditation. Clear your mind and focus on your breathing and listen for the voice of God

## At the End of Day 22

Describe your experience as being an intentional source of inspiration for others today.

Do you feel you inspired someone today, if even in a small way? If so explain. If not, why?

# Chapter 6

# A Week of Contribution

*"Give, and it shall be given unto you; good measure,*
*pressed down, and shaken together, and running over, shall*
*men give into your bosom. For with the same measure that*
*ye mete withal it shall be measured to you again."*
(Luke 6:38KJV)

Luke 6:38 is probably one of the most radical teachings in the Bible. I view it as radical because it is the only time Jesus promises His audience a blessing, where God is not the administrator of the blessing, but *men* are. It is radical also because this is the only time Jesus makes a promise that His audience will be blessed without requiring faithfulness to Him, but rather faithfulness to a system, principle, or a process. The point is that Jesus intimates that God has woven into the fabric of His creation principles that, if rejected, would cause doors of opportunity to be slammed shut and blessings forfeited. But if they are obeyed, the obedient would be placed in a position to get the most out of life.

Jesus begins this verse with the simple instruction to *give* or to contribute. This instruction to give is the divine protocol. When we engage in the act of selfless giving, we are imitating the very God who created us. God is a natural giver. He freely gave man a world loaded with everything he could ever want or need. Even after man's fall from grace, God continued to give. He continues to give His love to man. He gives him a way back to a perfect relationship with Him through the cross of Calvary. Jesus' entire ministry was defined by giving. He gave wine to a dried-out wedding party. He gave the fish and the loaves to a hungry multitude. He gave sight to the blind. He gave healing to the sick, and He gave restoration to the prodigal and pardon to the woman caught in adultery. Even while He was dying, He continued to give. He gave forgiveness to His enemies, paradise to a dying thief, and He gave John to His mother and gave His mother to John. After the resurrection, the last thing He did before He ascended to heaven was to breathe on His disciples to give them the Holy Ghost.

Everything in nature was created to freely give. The sun gives of its heat, light, and solar energy, for free. The oceans, seas, rivers, lakes, and creeks give of their sea food, at no cost. Springs don't charge for fresh drinking water. The clouds give freely of their rains. The trees give away their fruit and their leaves freely give oxygen.

Flowers don't charge for the privilege of gazing upon their beauty and enjoying their fragrance. Fields freely render their crops.

God also created mankind to be givers. After God created male and female, the first command they were given was to be fruitful and multiply, and to replenish the earth (Genesis 1:27-28). God commanded them to give of their bodies and minds to be a blessing to the earth and to mankind. God's original intent for mankind was to constantly live in the *give mode*. God wired mankind for giving. After God created mankind in the give mode, He said, *"It is good."* When Satan entered the picture, he convinced mankind to live out of the carnal nature rather out of God's original intent to live in the spiritual nature, thus taking became far more important than giving. In fact, the nature of the original sin involves taking. The serpent tempted Eve to *take* from the forbidden tree and eat. Since that day, man has been locked in the take mode. Even before birth, we are in the take mode. While in the womb, everything we get is taken from the mother. When we come from the womb, we are in the take mode. We are conditioned from infancy to believe that the way to happiness is through taking. Infants only take, without ever thinking about giving. In the infancy stage, humans do not have the mental or spiritual capacity to comprehend the concept of giving. They expect to take nourishment and protection from their caretakers. When infants' needs go unmet, they scream and cry until someone gives them what they want, whether it is food, attention, or comfort. Too often, this mentality carries over into childhood, teenage years, young adulthood, and throughout life, and over the course of time that mode hardens and becomes difficult to break.

## Emotional attachments

One of the great hindrances that prevents the transition from the take mode to the give mode is the emotional attachment to personal possessions. Our culture has seduced too many people into thinking that their identity and personhood are established by what they possess. Thus, we embrace things as an actual dimension of our being. That is, our things become an extension of our identity to the point that our possessions reflect who we are. In this mindset our cars, clothes, money, houses, and other personal possessions represent who we are.

We have become so emotionally attached to our possessions that we attribute human qualities, traits, and names to inanimate objects. We *genderize* our cars into females and then give them feminine names. I am guilty of naming my first car Betty, and would brag about how well *she* ran. B.B. King named his guitar Lucille. In the television show *The Knight Rider,* the car was named Kitt. It is an expected practice among yacht owners to name their boats, and often they are given female names.

I once counseled a young lady who complained about having no friends, and she had bad relationships with her family members. She was twice divorced, and her third marriage was on the rocks. She was a very troubled woman. She complained that she couldn't get anything from anyone. No one would give her money in spite of her financial straits. No one understood the hard times she was facing in her life, she complained. No one would *help her out*. She cried, *"I just can't get anyone to do anything for me!"* After forty-five minutes of listening to her complain about what everyone would not do for her, I asked, *"When was the last time you did something for someone other than yourself?"* She looked at me in utter bewilderment and asked, "What does that have to do with anything?" She continued, "I came to you for help and not a sermon. Save the preaching for the pulpit." I responded, "That's your problem. You are always looking for someone to do something for you and you never look to do anything for others. You look to family and friends to give you money, help, understanding, and love, but you never look to give these things. Even now, you are looking to me to give you something." She got up from her chair and headed to the door while remarking, "I did not come here to be talked to like a child. I came to you for help." This woman could not fathom the idea of giving. Giving was too much of a burden. She seemed hopelessly stuck in the *take mode*.

### Utilitarian attachment

A utilitarian attachment to things is to use a particular item as simply a means to an end, and nothing more. When there is a utilitarian attachment to things you tend to enjoy them more than when there is an emotional attachment. If you are emotionally attached to something, you are so concerned about losing it or damaging it that you never enjoy it. Thus, your things become a source of stress and tension rather than enjoyment. Some people have never enjoyed the house that they work hard to pay for. They are overly concerned about someone dropping sauce on the carpet or tracking dirt into the house, or someone dropping a pretzel in the couch cushions or getting fingerprints and smudge marks on the mirrors and windows. Their worries are compounded by obsessive concerns that somehow, some way, some day it might be taken away from them. There are countless stories of people who have won the lottery for millions of dollars, who admit that their lives were far better and less stressful before they won the millions. They are always on guard protecting their money. They are suspicious of everyone, because everyone is a potential con man or rip-off artist who is after their money. So they never enjoy it because they are so attached to it that their worst fear is to lose it.

When God gets us to the place where we can appreciate things for what they are and nothing more, by dissolving our emotional attachments to them, we are in the position to be what God created us to be, givers.

In His teaching, after Jesus gave the divine protocol He gave the divine promise, *and it shall be given unto you.* The object of this promise is anyone who dares to buy into it. If you embrace this promise and put the principles into practice, then you are the object of this promise. How exhilarating and exciting it was when it dawned on me that Jesus is speaking directly to me in Luke 6:38. When you really look at it, this passage is so personal and direct that it is equal to Jesus Himself writing this passage to you in a letter with your name and address on it! The powerful point of this passage is that this promise is yours for the claiming!

Practicing the principle is actually very simple: if you want joy, give joy to others. If you want love, learn to give love. If you want attention and appreciation, give attention and appreciation to others. If you want material affluence, help others to become materially affluent. In fact, the easiest way to get what you want is to help others get what they want. This principle works equally well for individuals, corporations, societies, and nations. "If you want to be blessed with all the good things in life, learn to silently bless everyone with all the good things in life."[26] The Apostle Paul certainly subscribes to this principle. He writes, "Remember this: Whoever sows sparingly will also reap sparingly, and whoever sows generously will also reap generously. Each man should give what he has decided in his heart to give, not reluctantly or under compulsion, for God loves a cheerful giver. And God is able to make all grace abound to you, so that in all things at all times, having all that you need you will abound in every good work" (2 Corinthians 9:6-8 KJV).

---

[26] Chopra, P. 31.

To break free from the take mode and transition to the give mode, you must begin to incorporate the act of giving as a daily part of your life, in fact live a life of giving. Give to all on a daily basis. Give kindness to all, give love to all, and give appreciation, compliments, forgiveness, and understanding to all constantly. This way you guarantee that you will constantly receive.

A member of my congregation recounts the following story that illustrates this principle with *goosebump* excitement! A struggling young single mom of two children was at the Greyhound bus station boarding a bus to go to a nearby city to visit family and friends. While at the bus station, she encountered a young woman with two children begging for money to purchase tickets to travel to the same city. The man she and her children were living with had put them out on the street. She was trying to get back to her hometown. My member was struggling financially herself, but she happened to have fifty extra dollars that she had won in a karaoke contest the night before. Fifty dollars was exactly what this lady at the bus station needed to put with the money she already had to buy three bus tickets for herself and her children. My member took her last fifty dollars and gladly gave it to her. My member said that she saw something in the lady at the bus station that reminded her of herself. They rode the bus together, laughing and talking all the way to their destination. Less than three months later, my member was going to be short on her mortgage payment because her job was slow in paying employees that particular pay period. A friend was at her house while she was talking on the phone to a representative at the mortgage company, explaining why her payment would be slow that month. When she got off the phone, this friend of hers took out her checkbook and wrote her a $1,000 check because she had overheard her telephone conversation. Her friend told her, "I just want to bless you because there is something about you that reminds me of myself." Coincidence? I think not — this is a divine principle at work.

# Monday Day 23

*"If in serving, let him serve."* (Romans 12:7NIV)

**Today's Challenge:** Commit or recommit to a ministry, auxiliary, or program functioning at your church.

Major news outlets around the country are reporting that volunteerism is on the decline in America. At one point in history, our country led the world in volunteerism. Many of the greatest organizations in the world were born here in America, and grew strong through volunteerism. Organizations like the Boy and Girl Scouts of America, the United Way, Goodwill Industries, the NAACP, YMCA, YWCA, and many more, are all great institutions that were built basically by volunteers. But today all of these wonderful institutions are either struggling or not nearly as strong as they used to be, because of waning volunteerism.

Unfortunately, the church has not escaped from being affected by this troubling phenomenon. The church is greatly affected because participation in the life of the church is viewed by too many as simply volunteering and not a spiritual vocation.

Until we consider ourselves what the Word considers us, and not what the world considers us, the church will struggle to be what God wants it to be. That is, we were never considered volunteers by the Word, that's a title the world gives to its unpaid workers. Moreover, we are considered servants of Christ by the Word. There is a major difference between a volunteer and a servant of Christ. A volunteer is someone working in an organization or for a cause without legal obligation or expectation of being paid.

What drives a volunteer to offer service? I have volunteered for many things in my life, and different issues drove me to volunteer for certain things. While I was in graduate school I volunteered my counseling and ministerial services to a program that cared for victims of domestic abuse. The fact that I grew up witnessing domestic violence firsthand, and saw how damaging it can be to families, drove me to volunteer for that ministry. Women who are victims of rape often become serious advocates for rape victims and volunteer their services to programs that care for such victims. There are people who wanted to be professional athletes, but didn't quite have what it took. They often end up volunteering, to vicariously live out their fantasy through others. I had a college professor who loved children but could never have any herself. She volunteered her services for many years at an orphanage.

Many different things drive volunteers to offer service. Volunteerism is a great thing, no matter what the driving forces are. However, many of the driving forces for volunteerism are selfish. I volunteered to counsel victims of domestic violence because of a personal need. My volunteering helped me work through personal issues. Once those issues had been resolved, there was no longer anything driving me to volunteer in that capacity, so I stopped working in the program. Perhaps victims of rape use their volunteerism as interventionists, as personal therapy to help them to heal from their horrendous ordeals. But when they experience healing and wholeness, their pain will no longer be a driving force. The volunteer coach is perhaps driven to accomplish something through his team or an individual athlete that he was never able to accomplish. Once that is accomplished, what then will be his motivation?

As servants of Jesus Christ, our drive is not selfish but selfless. We are not driven by pain or by unresolved issues. We are driven by our love and appreciation for Christ. When we are driven by love that never runs out, and motivated by our appreciation for Christ, that motivation never ends. This is what the Apostle Paul had in mind when he said, "I beseech you therefore, brethren, by the mercies of God, that ye present your bodies a living sacrifice, holy, acceptable unto God, which is your reasonable service." Paul informs us that it is the mercies of God that should be our ultimate motivation for rendering our service.

Let's make sure that the church is not victimized by inactivity the way the world's institutions have been. Let your motivation to offer service to your church be out of love for Christ, and the mercies of God!

**The Faith Challenge Day 23**

➤ 20-minute daily devotion.
  1. Scripture reading: Romans 12:2-12
  2. Prayer: a segment of your prayer should be that God will reveal to you in what area of the church you should serve.
  3. Meditation: 10-minute quiet meditation. Clear your mind and focus on your breathing and listen for the voice of God to provide direction for your life.
➤ Food fast from 8:00am to 8:00pm
➤ Today also abstain from the internet, television, radio, and any other form of electronic entertainment, unless of course it is required for your job.
➤ Prayer periods: 9:00am, 12:00pm, 3:00pm and 6:00pm. Your prayers should be for those you serve.

# At the End of Day 23

What organization within the church did you join today?

Describe how your involvement will enhance the organization.

# Tuesday Day 24

*"And Martha served."* (John 12:2KJV)

**Today's Challenge:** Today, offer your service to the church. Offer your time to help in the office, in janitorial service, youth ministry, senior ministry, food pantry or any area your church may need help.

We live in a generation where many people feel that the church is in existence to serve them, rather than they serve the church. In the 25th chapter of the Gospel of Matthew, Jesus makes it crystal clear that part of the ministry of the church is to meet the needs of the "least of these." In addition to this, Paul also informs us that the church has the responsibility to "Equip the saints, for the work of the ministry, for the edifying of the body of Christ." However, Jesus teaches that the greatest of all is not the one who is served but the one who serves the most (Luke 22:26)

In many cases, church employees are underpaid and overworked. Offering your service will help lighten the work load for the church staff and will greatly bless the church.

The carnal nature will resist this challenge because it cannot conceive of offering service without receiving anything tangible in exchange. The carnal will reason, "If the church staff is getting paid, why should I do this for free, I deserve a small stipend or at least a gift certificate for my effort."

To offer your service today with love and joy, not expecting any-thing tangible in return, is to know the true joy of service.

---

**The Faith Challenge Day 24**

➢ A 20-minute daily devotion
  1. Scripture reading: Ephesians 4:11-17
  2. Prayer: your prayer should include asking God in what capacity should you serve today.
  3. A 10-minute meditation: clear your mind and focus on your breathing and listen for the voice of God.
➢ Prayer periods: 9:00am, 12:00pm, 3:00pm and 6:00pm. Your prayers should be prayers of thanksgiving to God for allowing you to serve.
➢ If tonight is your church's mid-week worship night, you are to attend.

---

## At the End of Day 24

In what capacity did you offer your service to your church? Describe your experience.

Do you feel that God was pleased with your service today? Explain.

## Wednesday Day 25

*"What I want is for you to receive a well-earned reward because of your kindness (to me)."* (Philippians 4:17NLT)

**Today's Challenge:** Write down the reasons you are grateful to someone, then visit or contact that person to express your gratitude.

*Thank you* is such a powerful expression that it is often taken for granted by the very people who should be expressing it the most. Expressing gratitude is a humbling experience because by doing so you are acknowledging that you are the recipient of someone's favor. This is often difficult for the carnal to accept, because it never relates to others as equals. The carnal always sees itself as either superior or inferior to others. If it sees itself as superior, it relates to others in condescension. If it sees itself as inferior to others, it is intimidated by others and will either stay on the attack of others by constantly putting others down. Or, he constantly touts his accomplishments in the hopes of gaining approval. Or, he completely withdraws from others. The carnal would much rather be in a position of superiority. Therefore, it is difficult for the carnal nature to express gratitude to someone for showing kindness, because to express gratitude is to acknowledge that someone has done something for you. To the carnal nature, if someone does something for you it means that that person is superior to you, and to express gratitude is to acknowledge that person's superiority. So rather than losing superiority by expressing gratitude, the carnal nature will reason that it is really not a favor, but the kindness was owed and therefore releases the carnal nature of its obligation to express gratitude.

The carnal nature has robbed so many from true blessings because it works diametrically opposite to how this spiritual universe was designed to operate. The more gratitude you offer, the more people, situations, and things will be sent into your life to benefit you so that you can give thanks again and again. Have you ever noticed the people who give thanks the most have the most to give thanks for?

Think back over your life. Start with yesterday and go back as far as you can and think of someone who helped you the most. It may be a school teacher, someone from the old neighborhood, a friend, coworker, or whomever. Write down how this person blessed your life and then find the person and express your gratitude.

---

**The Faith Challenge Day 25**

➢ A 20-minute daily devotion
   1. Scripture reading: Philippians 4:12-19
   2. Prayer: your prayer should be a prayer of thanksgiving for all the people who have made positive contributions to your life.
   3. A 10-minute meditation: clear your mind and focus on your breathing and listen for the voice of God.
➢ Prayer periods: 9:00am, 12:00pm, 3:00pm and 6:00pm. Give thanks for those who have blessed you.
➢ If tonight is your church's mid-week worship night, you are to attend.

---

# At the End of Day 25

Who are the persons to whom you owe gratitude? What did the people/person do to help you?

How did you find the person?

How did the person receive your gesture of gratitude?

How did offering gratitude make you feel?

# Thursday Day 26

*"But when you give to the needy, do not let your left hand know what your right hand is doing."* (Matthew 6:3NIV)

**Today's Challenge:** Perform an act of kindness for someone anonymously.

To perform an anonymous act of kindness is one of the most carnal-less acts that one can perform. The carnal nature demands attention for doing good deeds for others. This attention makes the carnal person feel superior to the person receiving the help and often causes embarrassment for the recipient. Jesus was very much aware of the carnal nature's malignant desire for attention through helping others. That's why he warned His audience, "So when you give to the needy, do not announce it with trumpets, as the hypocrites do in the synagogues and on the streets, to be honored by men. I tell you the truth, they have received their reward in full…so that your giving may be in secret. Then your Father, who sees what is done in secret, will reward you" (Matthew 6:2-4NIV).

I will share a few powerful stories that I found on a wonderful website that documents the testimonies of those who have been the recipients of anonymous acts of kindness, and the extraordinary impact these acts had on their lives.

"I was in a McDonalds drive-through with my 3 kids getting something to eat the other day. When I drove up to the window the woman smiled, handed me a blue card and said 'the person in front of you paid for your food.' My first response was, 'are you sure?' And with an even bigger smile she said, 'I'm very sure.' WOW! Are you kidding? I am just astonished that someone would do that. Nothing like this ever happens to me. I haven't stopped smiling. My eldest daughter and I can't wait to pass it on somehow. Thank you."

—Kristen J.

"This was the beginning! Things only got better from here. On March 8, 2007 we received an envelope with two sets of instructions, maps, and tickets in it. Each set of instructions was to be opened at specific times and places. The first instructions and map took us to a pre-paid supper at a Celtic nightspot in Manchester, NH. After having supper and drinks, the waitress informed us that we could open our second set of instructions. Upon opening our second envelope, we discovered that we had been tagged to attend the performance of the Celtic Woman concert being held at the Manchester Verizon Wireless Arena that same evening. What a wonderful surprise!"

—Harvey & Caryn M.

"All I can say is, God bless you whoever you are. My husband and I have been working two jobs each for the past year to try and make ends meet. We live modestly at best and do what we can to support our two boys as best we can. We have a happy home and we are a good family. At the end of November my husband developed bronchitis which later turned into pneumonia. As a result, he was unable to work for just over 2 months. Even with insurance the medical costs were overbearing. We ended up falling behind in our mortgage and we were heading into foreclosure. My husband and I have spent many sleepless nights worrying about what would happen, where we would go and about our boys. I prayed and prayed that we would find a way out of this and looked to our church for worship and loving support. Two weeks ago we received a call from one of the church elders saying that the elders would like to come by and see us, and that he had something for us. It seemed quite unusual and we were pretty curious. When he came by he handed us a blank envelope and inside the envelope was this blue card and enough money for us to pay for two months of our mortgage. Tears immediately started down both of our faces. We didn't know what to say and were in complete disbelief. When I finally gained some composure to say thank you, we were told that they had just been asked to deliver the envelope. He wasn't sure who had done this, which just made me tear up even more. This amazingly generous act has allowed us to almost completely catch up and we can see some light at the end of the tunnel. God moves in very amazing ways and we are so very blessed. It is unbelievably nice to know that such kindness exists. Thank you, thank you from the bottom of our hearts. We will so definitely find a way to pass this on."

—Jodie & Kyle L.

Spend today performing an anonymous act of kindness.

---

**The Faith Challenge Day 26**
➤ A 20-minute daily devotion
   1. Scripture reading: Matthew 6:1-8
   2. Prayer: your prayer should be a prayer for the person you are performing the act of kindness for.
   3. A 10-minute meditation: clear your mind and focus on your breathing and listen for the voice of God.
➤ Prayer periods: 9:00am, 12:00pm, 3:00pm and 6:00pm. Give thanks for those whom you have chosen to bless.
➤ If tonight is your church's mid-week worship night, you are to attend.

---

## At the End of Day 26

Who did you perform an anonymous act of kindness for today?

Explain in detail the act of kindness and how you felt.

# Friday Day 27

*"Try to excel in gifts that build up the church."*
(I Corinthians 14:12NIV)

**Today's Challenge:** Freely offer your special talent to your church for a year.

Willie O. Willis was a trustee at the Angel Visit Baptist Church in Dunnsville, Virginia. This small church was my first pastoral assignment. Mr. Willis would often tell the story about a small church in rural Virginia that was in desperate need of a new church facility. This church was the only church in the community. The church was the pride of the community, even though everyone in the community didn't belong to the church. The church launched a fundraising campaign to build a new facility. Despite the church and community's best efforts, they fell far short of their goal. They scaled back the original plans as much as they could, but still could not afford to move forward with the project. The chairman of the Deacon Board worked in the construction industry as a project manager for more than 20 years. To save costs, he offered to manage the project free of charge. He knew several subcontractors with whom he had worked who were members of the church and the community. He was able to convince them that the only way to get the facility built was if these subcontractors would volunteer their expertise to the church. The church had enough cash on hand, and with a small loan from the bank was able to purchase all of the materials for the building. Eighty percent of the work was done by volunteers from the church and community.

Upon completion of the project, many of the volunteers who worked on the building became dedicated members of the church. Mr. Willis recalled that many of the volunteers were reluctant at first, and only volunteered their services because of their loyalty to the deacon chairman. He had used many of these subcontractors when other project managers wouldn't use them. They felt that if they wanted to do more business with him in the future, they needed to respond to his request. But as the project moved forward, they began to understand that their contribution was worth much more than the money they could have made. When they realized the impact that their contribution was making on the church and community, they knew that they were being used by God. Their volunteerism became a spiritual practice. Many of the workers enhanced their relationship with God. Some who had never had a relationship with God developed one. The entire community experienced a powerful revival simply through these men freely freely offered their service.

**The Faith Challenge Day 27**

➤ A 20-minute daily devotion
  1. Scripture reading: Matthew 25:14-30
  2. Prayer: you should pray that the Lord will inspire you to offer your special talent to the church and that your contribution might bring glory to His name.
  3. A 10-minute meditation: clear your mind and focus on your breathing and listen for the voice of God.

➤ Prayer periods: 9:00am, 12:00pm, 3:00pm and 6:00pm. Give thanks for those whom you have chosen to bless.

# At the End of Day 27

What special talent did you offer to your church?

Do you foresee anything that might keep you from completely honoring your commitment?

Write your reflections:

## Saturday Day 28

*"Lord, the half of my goods I give to the poor."*
(Luke 19: 8 KJV)

**Today's Challenge:** Go through all of your possessions that you no longer use and share them with others.

There is an interesting episode that transpired in the 12th Chapter of the Gospel of Luke. A young man comes to Jesus with a complaint about his older brother who was in possession of the inheritance left by their father. The older brother would not share it with the younger brother. The older brother was not legally obligated to share it with the younger brother; otherwise, the younger brother could have taken the older brother to court and had a judge rule. But he felt his brother was morally obligated to share it, so he went to a rabbi, because this young man wanted Jesus to use His rabbinical authority to make a ruling on his behalf. Rather than rendering a ruling in the younger brother's favor, Jesus started teaching a lesson on the various kinds of greed. The bigger issue was not that the older brother would not share the inheritance, but that it was greed. Both the older brother and the younger brother were greedy. The older brother demonstrated his greed by not sharing with his brother, and younger brother demonstrated his greed by wanting more than what he needed. Greed is the hallmark of the carnal nature.

The carnal nature finds its identity in the abundance of things. The more the carnal nature has, the more significant and secure it feels. That is why it is difficult to get carnal-dominated people to part with their material things, because the fewer things that the carnal has the less significant it feels.

Today's Faith Challenge is breaking away from greed's carnal grip by giving away things you don't use anymore. The carnal nature will resist by trying to convince you that "you never know when you'll need this or that." If you haven't used it in all this time, it is not likely you are going to need it. And even if there comes time when you do need it, you will have set a universal spiritual law in motion that at the time you need it, you'll have it.

---

**The Faith Challenge Day 28**

➤ A 20-minute daily devotion
   1. Scripture reading: Luke 19:1-9
   2. Prayer: your prayer should be that God will direct you into giving your possessions to someone who needs them.
   3. A 10-minute meditation: clear your mind and focus on your breathing and listen for the voice of God to provide you with instruction on whom you should offer your possessions.
➤ Prayer periods: 9:00am, 12:00pm, 3:00pm and 6:00pm. Give thanks to God for giving you the faith to give into the lives of others.

---

## At the End of Day 28

Were you able to give away things you don't use anymore? If not, why?

What and to whom did you give?

Was it difficult to give it away? If yes, why?

How did giving things away make you feel?

# Sunday Day 29

*"Bring ye all the tithes into the storehouse."* (Malachi 3:10KJV)

**Today's Challenge:** Go to worship and pay your tithes.

Tithing is not a money issue, it is a spiritual issue. Those who are encapsulated in the carnal find it impossible to give 10% of their hard-earned income to the church for ongoing expenses of the ministry. I have been at my church for more than twenty years and I have seen people agonize over this divine idea of paying a tithe to the church. There have been many who were never able to overcome this struggle. The real struggle is not with the money, but with the carnal nature.

Tithing is purely a spiritual act. The main reason we are to pay a tithe is because God said it. Tithing is an act of obedience to God. Tithing also sets in motion the forces of the spiritual world to work on your behalf. God promised in His Word that when we tithe "He would open the windows of heaven and pour you out a blessing you don't have enough room to receive." When He refers to opening the windows and pouring out a blessing, He is talking about sending rain to the land. His audience is agricultural workers. In the farming industry, rain is a must. No matter how hard the famer works to prepare and cultivate his field, and plant his seed, if there is no rain it is all in vain. The promise is that when the farmer pays a tithe to the Lord as a spiritual act of obedience, God would send rain to their fields and bless their hard work with success. God also promised that He would "Rebuke the devourer for their sakes." After the farmer sows the seed and the harvest comes in, sometimes the locusts and other pests would swarm the fields and destroy the crops for the season, sometimes sending the farmer into deep poverty for the year. It would sometimes take the farmer years to recover from such an infestation. But God promised that if the farmer displays his obedience by giving a tithe, God would rebuke the devourer for him.

In giving a tithe to the church, we bless God by demonstrating obedience to Him. We also bless ourselves by putting ourselves in the position to be blessed by God. By giving a tithe we also bless the church, the community, and the world. We bless the church by putting it in a position to carry out the ministry of the church. When the church is carrying out its mission, the community is blessed because the gospel is spread.

Your challenge today is to break free of the carnal and give a tithe to your church, and be a blessing to all parties involved.

---

**The Faith Challenge Day 29**

➢ 20-minute daily devotion
  1. Scripture reading: Malachi 3:6-12
  2. Prayer: Give thanks to God for allowing you to tithe and ask God to send his blessings into your life.
  3. Meditation: 10-minute quiet meditation. Clear your mind and focus on your breathing and listen for the voice of God

# At the End of Day 29

Did you give a tithe to your church today? If not, why?

How did giving a tithe make you feel?

Is this a practice you are willing to continue? If not, why?

## Monday Day 30

*"Giving thanks always for all things unto God and the*
*Father in the name of our Lord Jesus Christ."*
(Ephesians 5:20KJV)

**Today's Faith Challenge:** Give God thanks all day in all things.

Giving God thanks in all things is to acknowledge that He is in control and has your best interest at heart. If there is a door of opportunity closed in your face today, just know that God is involved in the process and is working for your good. If you receive some bad news or have an unpleasant encounter today, be aware that God already had this in His plan from the foundation of the world, and He already knows the end of the situation before it starts. Nothing sneaks up on God.

If Joseph had only seen what the Lord was doing in his life, he would have been giving thanks to God from the time his brother threw him into the pit and left him for dead, to the time he was promoted to the top position in Egypt. Since we have the benefit of the Holy Scripture we know that just because things don't go the way we want them to go does not mean that God is not involved. To the contrary, God is always intimately involved in every aspect of our lives, and when we constantly give thanks to God for everything we heighten our own awareness of His presence and participation. Paul said, "And we know that God works all things together for good for those who love God and those who are the called according to His purpose" (Romans 8:28KJV).

---

**The Faith Challenge Day 30**

➤ A 20-minute daily devotion
 1. Scripture reading: Psalm 136
 2. Prayer: your prayer should consist of a list of things that you can give God thanks for.
 3. A 10-minute meditation: clear your mind and focus on your breathing and listen for the voice of God.
➤ Prayer periods: 9:00am, 12:00pm, 3:00pm and 6:00pm. Give thanks for all He has done in your life.

---

# At the End of Day 30

Discuss four things you gave thanks to God for today.

How did continually giving God thanks affect your day?

# Conclusion

During the Faith Challenge there may have been some days that you were not able to participate. This may be a good time for you to go back and complete any missed assignments. If you have completed all of the assignments, congratulations! I hope you were successful at moving deeper into your relationship with God and that you are more aware of His presence throughout your day. I hope now, if you haven't already, begin to experience God's fellowship beyond corporate worship at church but as a moment by moment experience everyday of your life.

The intention of the Faith Challenge is also to heighten self awareness. If you took this challenge seriously you discovered some new realities about yourself, some that are good and some not so good. At least you know what areas in your life needs improving.

The Faith Challenge is not a 30 day fad but it is designed to change your life. I hope that you will incorporate some of these daily challenges into your life on permanent basis. Allow God's power to clear up your spiritual field and put you in the position to have the desires of your heart miraculous manifest in your life.

CPSIA information can be obtained at www.ICGtesting.com
Printed in the USA
LVOW060910150911

246320LV00002B/1/P